WALKIN

LAKELA

Ambleside — the South

Paul Hannon

HILLSIDE

HILLSIDE GUIDES - ACROSS THE NORTH

Long Distance Walks
- COAST TO COAST WALK   •DALES WAY   •CLEVELAND WAY
- WESTMORLAND WAY   •FURNESS WAY   •CUMBERLAND WAY
- LADY ANNE'S WAY   •PENDLE WAY   •NORTH BOWLAND TRAVERSE

Hillwalking - Lake District
- LAKELAND FELLS - SOUTH   •LAKELAND FELLS - EAST
- LAKELAND FELLS - NORTH   •LAKELAND FELLS - WEST

Circular Walks - Peak District
- NORTHERN PEAK   •EASTERN PEAK   •CENTRAL PEAK
- SOUTHERN PEAK   • WESTERN PEAK

Circular Walks - Yorkshire Dales
- HOWGILL FELLS   •THREE PEAKS   •MALHAMDALE
- WHARFEDALE   •NIDDERDALE   •WENSLEYDALE   •SWALEDALE

Circular Walks - North York Moors
- WESTERN MOORS   •SOUTHERN MOORS   •NORTHERN MOORS

Circular Walks - South Pennines
- BRONTE COUNTRY   •CALDERDALE   •ILKLEY MOOR

Circular Walks - Lancashire
- BOWLAND   •PENDLE & THE RIBBLE   • WEST PENNINE MOORS

Circular Walks - North Pennines
- TEESDALE   •EDEN VALLEY

Yorkshire Pub Walks
- HARROGATE/WHARFE VALLEY   •HAWORTH/AIRE VALLEY

Large format colour hardback

FREEDOM OF THE DALES

BIKING COUNTRY
- YORKSHIRE DALES CYCLE WAY   •WEST YORKSHIRE CYCLE WAY
- MOUNTAIN BIKING - WEST & SOUTH YORKSHIRE
- AIRE VALLEY BIKING GUIDE   •CALDERDALE BIKING GUIDE
- GLASGOW Clyde Valley & Loch Lomond

- **YORK WALKS** *City Theme Walks*

- **WALKING COUNTRY TRIVIA QUIZ** *Over 1000 questions*

Send for a detailed current catalogue and pricelist

WALKING COUNTRY

LAKELAND FELLS
Ambleside & the South

Paul Hannon

HILLSIDE

HILLSIDE
PUBLICATIONS
11 Nessfield Grove
Keighley
West Yorkshire
BD22 6NU

First published 1998

© Paul Hannon 1998

ISBN 1 870141 60 1

Whilst the author has walked and researched all of the routes for the purposes of this guide, no responsibility can be accepted for any unforeseen circumstances encountered while following them. The publisher would, however, greatly appreciate any information regarding material changes, and any problems encountered.

Cover illustrations: Langdale Pikes from Loughrigg;
Easedale Tarn and Helvellyn from Blea Rigg
Back cover: Froswick from across Kentmere
(Paul Hannon/Big Country Picture Library)

Page 1: Wansfell, looking to Caudale Moor and Thornthwaite Crag
Page 3: Loughrigg Fell, looking to Seat Sandal,
Dollywaggon Pike and Great Rigg

Printed in Great Britain by
Carnmor Print & Design
95-97 London Road
Preston
Lancashire
PR1 4BA

CONTENTS

INTRODUCTION

The fells of the Lake District are the most impressive and most popular in England. The majority of the National Park's 866 square miles is dominated by its hills, from the rocky fastnesses of Scafell Pike, the summit of England, down to some delightful low-level fells. To do justice to this unique landscape, 100 outstanding fellwalks have been devised and shared among a series of four definitive guidebooks. Together these embrace the best fellwalking in the country, and each guide deals with a logically defined area of Lakeland.

The walks within this volume cover the southern part of the National Park, with Ambleside the focal point. The most popular bases are Grasmere, Langdale and Coniston, and some of the best known fells include Bowfell, Coniston Old Man and the Langdale Pikes. The three companion guides feature Patterdale & the East; Keswick & the North; and Buttermere & the West.

Although any number of more demanding walks can be planned by enthusiasts, the aim of this series is to provide a varied range of outings within the scope of most walkers. Thus a limit of around 10 miles and 3500 feet of ascent per walk has been set: most walks are in fact well within these bounds. A feature of these walks is their variety, so that ridgewalks alternate with valley approaches, there are steep climbs, gentle climbs, routes that include mountain tarns and waterfalls. All share the character that makes the Lakeland Fells so special.

The great majority of the Lakeland Fells is freely open to walkers, though many of the routes described are in any case on public rights of way. Any access routes onto the hills are always on rights of way or permitted routes. Please be sensitive when passing near farms and dwellings, and if you must take a dog with you, ensure it is on a lead. While we may have every right to be there, the sheer weight of our numbers means it is particularly important to also act responsibly.

Mountain safety is a subject dealt with in several chunky volumes, and here it should be sufficient to say that the most important elements are to be properly equipped, and realistically aware of the three great limitations of time, physical condition and weather. An ability to use map and compass is strongly recommended, as one can be easily disorientated in mist. In winter conditions the fells take on an entirely different character. In such circumstances even the humblest of fells present new dangers: ice, snow, bitterly cold or gale force winds, and

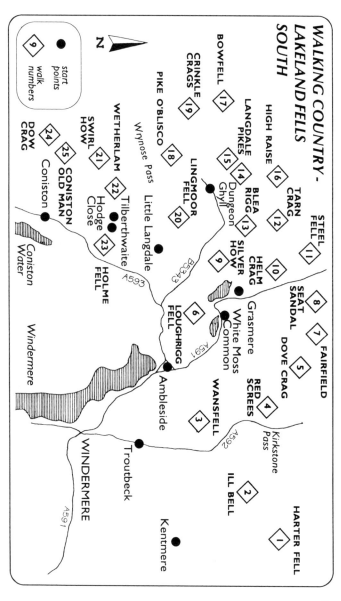

WALKING COUNTRY -
LAKELAND FELLS
SOUTH

N

start points

walk numbers

short daylight hours all demand greater preparation. In true winter conditions one should carry ice axe and crampons and be competent in their use. Don't be put off the winter experience, however, for it is in this season that the fells are seen at their most stunningly beautiful.

The overwhelming popularity of these hills is all too evident to those who set foot upon them. Many paths are worn wide and bare, and in most parts of the district evidence of repair work will be encountered. In recent years this has grown into a major undertaking, with the National Park and the National Trust at the forefront. In most cases the paths are sensitively restored with stone surfaces, a dramatic improvement on the ugly scars they replace. Wherever possible please adhere to the paths old and new, and to any diversions during ongoing pathwork. Additionally, walkers can show respect for our fragile hills by faithfully following zigzags and avoiding insensitive short-cuts; not descending at speed; not walking the fells in enormous groups; and by wearing the lightest footwear that doesn't jeopardise safety.

Most of the walks begin from villages or recognised parking areas, but please be sure not to obstruct local access. Many walks can also be accessed by public transport, so even if you came to the district by car, consider the local bus whenever possible in order not to exacerbate peak season traffic congestion. Stagecoach Cumberland produces an annual timetable which includes numerous seasonal services.

Using the guide
Each walk is self-contained, featuring essential details, sketch map, and route description including comment on features along the way. The basic maps serve merely to identify the location of the routes, for which a 1:25,000 scale map is strongly recommended. Best known for their excellent detail are the Ordnance Survey Outdoor Leisure maps, of which four cover the Lake District:-

4 - *English Lakes North West*   5 - *English Lakes North East*
6 - *English Lakes South West*   7 - *English Lakes South East*
(5, 6 and 7 are used in this guide, 6 and 7 being the principal ones)

Useful for general planning purposes are the Landranger maps at 1:50,000, and two sheets cover the area:
90 - Penrith, Keswick & Ambleside; 96 - Barrow in Furness & South Lakeland

The increasingly popular Harvey Maps also cover the district, and their 1:25,000 scale Superwalker maps are available as follows:
North West Lakeland   Western Lakeland   Northern Lakeland
Eastern Lakeland   Southern Lakeland   Central Lakeland

SOME USEFUL ADDRESSES

Ramblers' Association 1/5 Wandsworth Road, London SW8 2XX
Tel. 0171-339 8500

Lake District National Park Visitor Centre
Brockhole, Windermere (on A591)   Tel. 015394-46601

National Park/Tourist Information

Market Cross **Ambleside**	Tel. 015394-32582
Glebe Road **Bowness**	Tel. 015394-42895
Main Car Park **Coniston**	Tel. 015394-41533
Redbank Road **Grasmere**	Tel. 015394-35245
Main Car Park **Waterhead**	Tel. 015394-32729
Victoria Street **Windermere**	Tel. 015394-46499

Public Transport
Cumbria Journey Planner - Tel. 01228-606000
National Rail Enquiries - Tel. 0345-484950

Lake District Weather - Tel. 017687-75757

Lake District National Park Authority
Murley Moss, Oxenholme Rd, Kendal LA9 7RL Tel. 01539-724555

Cumbria Tourist Board
Ashleigh, Holly Road, Windermere LA23 2AQ   Tel. 015394-44444

Friends of the Lake District
No.3, Yard 77, Highgate, Kendal LA9 4ED   Tel. 01539-720788

The National Trust North West Regional Office
The Hollens, Grasmere, Ambleside LA22 9QZ   Tel. 015394-35599

The Country Code
- Respect the life and work of the countryside
- Protect wildlife, plants and trees
- Keep to public paths across farmland
- Safeguard water supplies
- Go carefully on country roads
- Keep dogs under control • Guard against all risks of fire
- Fasten all gates • Leave no litter - take it with you
- Make no unnecessary noise
- Leave livestock, crops and machinery alone
- Use gates and stiles to cross fences, hedges and walls

1 HARTER FELL

```
            SUMMITS
HARTER FELL    2552ft/778m
KENTMERE PIKE    2395ft/730m
SHIPMAN KNOTTS    1926ft/587m
```

START Kentmere   **Grid ref.** NY 456040

DISTANCE 10 miles/16km   **ASCENT** 2275ft/694m

ORDNANCE SURVEY MAPS
1:50,000 - Landranger 90   1:25,000 - Outdoor Leisure 7

ACCESS *Start from the church on a knoll in the centre of the scattered settlement. There is very limited parking by the church and institute, and an honesty box in the institute wall: please be careful not to block any gateways nor to restrict access along the road. At times a field by the bridge just before the church is opened for parking. A bus service operates from Kendal via Crook and Staveley on Summer weekends.*

This easy fellwalk offers a nice balance of valley and fell, linked by a classic mountain pass. The Nan Bield Pass was much used in packhorse days, and in Kentmere evidence of the old trade route can still be found in stone guideposts.

S Take a narrow lane immediately to the right of the church, and almost at once fork right on a rougher track. This runs on above a house (Rawe) to a junction of ways in front of another old farmhouse, Rook Howe. Alongside it the track continues on by a bouldery pasture. Ahead is our return high level ridge. Dropping down, look for a stile on the right giving access to a footbridge on the youthful and refreshingly clear river Kent.

Bear left up the colourful pasture behind the river to a stile onto the narrow walled bridleway of Low Lane. Go left, running grandly on to emerge into a field and stream crossing. Keep left on the more inviting level green way. A glorious panorama forms ahead as the Ill Bell ridge takes shape, with Froswick, to its right, usurping its parent fell. Meeting a firmer track, rise right with this, but as it climbs to the cluster of buildings at Hollowbank, keep left on a lower level enclosed way. Emerging, it rises to Overend.

Follow the drive out, but as it doubles back, ignore both this and the continuing rough lane. Alongside it are signs old and modern, the former being a characterful slate one pointing to Mardale. Cross over the lane as directed and rise gently on a green way, swinging left along the wall-top. This old bridleway runs parallel with the lane below. From a gate in a wall corner keep straight on, rising only gently before arriving at a ford and gate in the final wall. Rainsborrow Crag on Yoke is well seen across the valley, but Ill Bell itself remains the near permanent highlight.

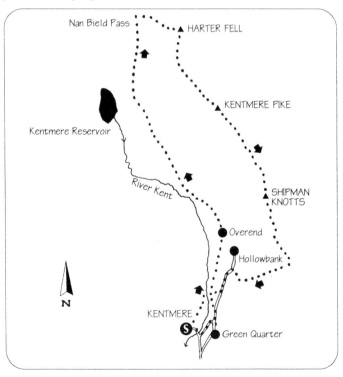

At last some climbing begins, rising through reeds then bracken onto a knoll. Keep straight on, noting an old quarry gash with spoil below it over to the right, while to its left is the prominent boulder of the Ull Stone. As the way runs gently on, a first glimpse of Kentmere Reservoir is obtained, then the path rises again to a knoll on the shoulder of Smallwaite Knott. This is a super spot, the way continuing as a true mountain path with a grand atmosphere. At the same time the summit of the Nan Bield Pass appears ahead, framed by rocky outcrops on the descending ridges.

A long, steady rise precedes a final, inevitable pull on faithfully retained zigzags. With rocky ground closing in on both sides, the narrow defile is gained suddenly and dramatically. A sturdy shelter occupies the spot, a unique feature for a Lakeland pass: the names *Mardale* and *Kentmere* are etched into it. Arrival on the finest of all Lakeland's passes is a cracking moment, with a glimpse of Haweswater duly revealed to the north.

This is a major walkers' crossroads, the onward route descending sharply by Small Water to Mardale Head and the left branch climbing over Mardale Ill Bell to High Street. To the right our path starts an immediate climb over the upper contours of Harter Fell. This arm extending down to the pass offers an enjoyable pull up the broken slopes, with super views down to Haweswater and back over the pass to one of the most inspiring mountain scenes in the district, High Street's eastern face split by the staircase ridge of Rough Crag.

The climb ends abruptly with a grassy stroll over a pathless plateau to a wrought-iron embellished summit cairn. Surprisingly Harter Fell's attractions do not extend to its summit, whose bizarre cairn is insufficient recompense for the grassy plateau denying any intimate views from this, Lakeland's easternmost 2500-footer. For the return to Kentmere trace the fence south over the broad spine of the mountain. A short drop to a double depression precedes an equally short climb (fence and wall share their duties along this ridge), now with a wall to the broad summit of Kentmere Pike; an Ordnance column stands just over the wall. The Lakeland skyline to the west is made to look very distant by the proximity of the well proportioned Ill Bell ridge, where Red Screes' craggy face slots neatly in between Ill Bell and Froswick.

Leaving the top, Shipman Knotts appears below as a wall corner is reached. Extensive views of both Longsleddale and Kentmere greet the eye, with both valleys equally well seen; note also the characterful bumps and ridges of the unfrequented eastern valleys beyond Longsleddale. As a fence takes over, the path drops more decisively down: when the fence turns off to run out to the top of Goat Scar (a splendid Longsleddale viewpoint), the path goes straight on down to a prominent wall-stile, before the slight rise onto Shipman Knotts. This minor top is also split by a wall, with a tiny cairn on its eastern side. Typical of many of Lakeland's subsidiary tops, this could be passed almost without notice on descent, yet would make a worthwhile target during an ascent. Over to the left are Tarn Crag and Grey Crag, probably the least known 2000-footers in Lakeland.

From here the path finally gets to grips with the descent, a wholly enjoyable business which ultimately brings arrival at the highest point of the old byway linking Kentmere with Sadgill, in Longsleddale. There are a few rougher moments as steeper ground alternates with marshy terrain. Turning right, this cart track ambles gently down to enter pastures at the barns of Stile End, then drops down to meet a narrow road to Hollowbank. Go left, and just after it becomes enclosed at a gate, take a stile on the right. A green path descends the colourful pasture to another stile back onto Low Lane. Either take the stile opposite to descend to the river and finish the walk as it began, or go left to rejoin the road, and on to a junction before the hamlet of Green Quarter. Turn right to wind steeply down to emerge onto the valley road at the bridge, with the church on its knoll just above.

Ill Bell, Froswick and High Street across Kentmere, from the return path at Stile End

```
┌─────────────────────────────┐
│          SUMMITS            │
│    YOKE     2316ft/706m     │
│  ILL BELL   2484ft/757m     │
│  FROSWICK   2362ft/720m     │
└─────────────────────────────┘
```

START Troutbeck   **Grid ref.** NY 413028

DISTANCE 10 miles/16km   **ASCENT** 2575ft/785m

ORDNANCE SURVEY MAPS
1:50,000 - Landranger 90   1:25,000 - Outdoor Leisure 7

ACCESS Start from Troutbeck Church, on the A592 Windermere-Patterdale road east of the village centre. There is a parking area just up the lane by Church Bridge. Seasonal weekend bus service from Bowness to Glenridding (daily in high summer).

The shapely summit cone of Ill Bell is one of the more familiar features of south-eastern Lakeland. Identified in countless views with the help of its satellite Froswick, it is just as good on top as it looks from the valley: a top to savour.

S From Church Bridge the main road is followed briefly south (bridging Trout Beck) before turning off up the rough lane on the left: this is the start of the Garburn Road, once an important route into Kentmere. After a steep pull it swings left and, incorporating two other rough roads, follows an unswerving course to gradually gain height above the Troutbeck valley: our three hills are well arrayed, leading to Thornthwaite Crag at the back. Keen eyes will discern the slanting groove on Froswick's flank that is the Scot Rake, on our return route.

A long climb passes beneath small plantations and an old quarry, and only after a considerable time is the top of the pass neared. By now the shapely pair have disappeared behind Yoke, though the views westward remain little changed, featuring a tremendous skyline of fells from Coniston Old Man round to Langdale. On the top a gate admits to open ground. At the first bend a cairn sends our path off to the left before reaching the true summit of the pass. Initially cairned, the path retains the gentle character of the climb, and enjoys a grassy stride for half a mile on an old quarrymans' way around the western flank. Remain on this main way which ignores a branch right just after a sidestream. Ultimately it swings across a peaty shelf to gain the wall climbing the ridge from the top of the pass. The first views east reveal the Harter Fell ridge, and the Kentmere valley down below.

Just a little higher, the wall parts company at a stile, and a steeper section is quickly completed to espy a beckoning cairn. En route to it the going eases to arrive at a fork: the left path opts to contour to avoid the summit of Yoke, while that on the right does the honourable thing and pays it a visit. The summit cairn stands just a minute beyond the false one. The summit panorama can be enhanced by strolling a few yards north to the edge of a gully, to gain a bird's-eye view of Kentmere Reservoir. Equally impressively, the dark cone of Ill Bell appears to be just a stone's throw away.

From Yoke the path continues north across a minor dip to quickly attain the summit of Ill Bell. The location is never in doubt, for it is bedecked with two notable cairns, with a third, more graceful one being a superb viewpoint for Windermere. Thanks to its lack of areal extent, nothing is lost in dull foreground, and the panorama falls into four distinct categories: westwards is a fine array of mountains, with all the giants finding a place in the frame; further north are the smoother outlines of Helvellyn and its high supporting ridges;

FROSWICK

Scot Rake

ILL BELL

YOKE

Troutbeck Park

N

Garburn Pass

△ Sallows

△ Sour Howes

A592

TROUTBECK

S

close at hand is the immense bulk of Ill Bell's colleagues in the High Street range, while the scene is completed by a wide sweep of the Pennines and Morecambe Bay in the south-east.

Ill Bell's favourite of its two satellites is Froswick, just over half a mile to the north and made in its own likeness. Descend to the small col and ignoring the ubiquitous contouring path, follow the main path up the grassy ridge, skirting impressive drops into the upper Kentmere valley to gain its tidy summit. Destined to forever stand in the shadow of its parent fell, its endearing little top enjoys similar views, though Windermere is upstaged by an enticing glimpse of Ullswater slotting snugly into the gap of Threshthwaite Mouth.

From Froswick the path effects a rapidly accomplished descent to the saddle before Thornthwaite Crag. Just 50 yards up it, however, a thin trod slants off to the left, rising to join the green course of the Scot Rake: alternatively, simply stroll down the grassy slope from the saddle to join it. The old way was the route by which the High Street Roman road took to the heights to link forts at Galava (Ambleside) and Brocavum (Brougham, near Penrith): the name Scot Rake later appended suggests it was used by raiders from across the border. This old grooved track now leads unfailingly and rapidly back down into the valley of Hagg Gill, with every step a delight.

At the bottom a bridle-gate in a wall junction sees us off the fell proper, and a fainter way continues straight down the reedy pasture. This soon becomes a firm track in the company of Hagg Gill before swinging right to run along the base of Troutbeck Tongue. A wall provides company most of the way, and gradually the view back to Threshthwaite Mouth is lost as we pass beneath two old quarry sites across the beck. On emerging beyond the Tongue, the track swings sharp right to approach the farm at Troutbeck Park, just ahead. Here cut a corner by taking a gate in the wall that joins in, and head straight down the field. Continue on to the far end to join the access road by a bridge and confluence with Trout Beck.

This surfaced farm road now leads all the way back. Behind, our three hills have regained their shape, as we cross the high arched Ing Bridge and look down on a crystal clear stream. As the road turns to climb to the cottages at Town Head, just above, an enclosed bridleway to the left will lead more directly onto the road, with the church just down to the left. Alternatively, the farm road climbs to the cluster at Town Head where the *Queens Head* offers a well-earned conclusion.

SUMMITS	
WANSFELL PIKE	1588ft/484m
WANSFELL	1597ft/487m

START *Ambleside*   **Grid ref.** *NY 376045*

DISTANCE *8 miles/13km*   **ASCENT** *1700ft/518m*

ORDNANCE SURVEY MAPS
1:50,000 - Landranger 90   1:25,000 - Outdoor Leisure 7

ACCESS *Start from the Market Place. There are several car parks. Served by bus from Windermere, Kendal and Keswick.*

In the company of higher fells Wansfell never feels overlooked, and this proud guardian of Windermere is a deservedly popular objective from the bustling little town at the head of the lake.

S Leave the Market Place by the side road running past Barclays Bank onto a back road. This is Stock Ghyll Lane, signposted left behind the *Salutation Hotel* 'to the waterfalls'. Stock Ghyll flows alongside, and Wansfell Pike appears up above. When the beck parts company, a path shadows it into the woodland of Stockghyll Park. When the path forks keep on the near side of the beck, climbing past several viewing stations for the spectacular cataracts of Stock Ghyll Force (see page 23). On gaining the top of the falls, turn right on a level path doubling back to leave the wood at an antiquated turnstile.

Emerging back onto the lane, resume left, crossing a cattle-grid to emerge into the open, looking far up the valley of Stock Ghyll. Ahead, the bulk of Red Screes overlooks the tiny dot of the *Kirkstone Pass Inn*, and a surfaced drive to Grove Farm heads away. Within a minute a stile on the right marks the commencement of the ascent proper. A path climbs a field to the terminus of a green lane, then continues more punishingly up the uniformly steep flanks. The benefits of this are the opportunities to halt and savour the extensive views unfolding.

Beyond the town is a mountain skyline from Coniston Old Man to Red Screes, featuring the Coniston Fells, Crinkle Crags, Bowfell, Langdale Pikes, High Raise and the Fairfield Horseshoe. Much path restoration is encountered, and towards the top occasional rock outcrops are passed before the ridge-wall is seen in front. Don't advance to the ladder-stile in it, but scramble left up the small rocky knoll of Wansfell Pike, and find a perch. The bird's-eye view is one of the finest! Only on gaining the top does Windermere appear, and in a big way, while the unfolding panorama of the ascent can now be enjoyed at leisure. With less than a quarter of the walk completed, all the work is done.

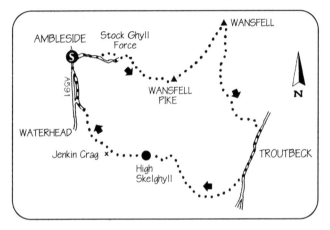

The actual cairn stands across the fence that spans the top, but this matters little as this is not the true summit of the fell. It is, however, as far as most people venture, so while the unadventurous head straight down on the well-blazed path continuing the line of the climb, cross the stile and turn left with a thin path along the beckoning ridge. At the end stands the unsung summit of Wansfell, and this broad, undulating ridge allows us to take full advantage of the height already gained.

Almost at once a wall replaces the fence, and a very pleasant walk ensues, drawn on by the shapely Ill Bell ridge beyond our objective, and with Red Screes exerting its full stature to the left. Beyond an intervening wall and subsequent rise, the ridge-wall trends left of the true watershed, but a slender path remains true to the height of land. Soon the summit is gained, marked by a cairn on a grassy knoll, with another wall appearing just below.

This main top conveys a distinct impression of being more at home nearer its real family, the Troutbeck fells (see illustration on page 1). The descent from the cairned summit commences by doubling sharply back to the right, the sketchiest of paths being admirably served by a series of cleverly sited cairns on prominent alps. These lead down to a wall, at the point where it converts into a green lane.

This is the head of Nanny Lane, which can be followed without further ado down into the scattered village of Troutbeck. This walled byway is an absolute charmer, being green and lush for most of the way, during which time it absorbs the direct descent path from the Pike. It culminates as a rutted watercourse that can only do a sound job in deterring potential illegal users from gaining and ruining the delectable upper sections.

Noting first that Troutbeck's two licensed premises are along to the left, the walk turns right along the road. A fair portion of the village is experienced, noting several roadside wells and some fine individual houses before reaching the Institute and Post office with its faded wooden sign on the wall corner. A little further on the road is the 17th century statesman's house at Townend (National Trust), just short of which a walled path can be used to climb back up to the main route, which is the rough lane branching up to the right from the Institute.

This is Robin Lane, a grand byway that climbs at length but only gently as it swings round Wansfell's southern flanks. On levelling out a vast portion of Windermere shimmers over to the left. 200 yards beyond a pillar up to the right, the lane is vacated at a profusely signed gate on the left: at this point, ahead, the summit ridge of this colourful fell returns to view in fine style. A good path now takes up the journey, curving down through a couple of pastures to a bridge where a surfaced drive climbs to High Skelghyll Farm, in view for some time.

From a gate beyond the farmhouse a wide track runs along to enter Skelghyll Wood. Descending through it, soon a sign indicates the branch path to Jenkin Crag, a celebrated Windermere viewpoint just yards to the left. The broad path, meanwhile, continues down through the trees, swinging right to bridge lively Stencher Beck. It soon bears right again to run a level course out of the trees, with views now over Waterhead to the Coniston and Langdale fells. Merging into a drive and then a lane, the way descends onto Old Lake Road as it is about to join the main road through Ambleside. Turn right along this quieter back road for a lengthy stride back into the centre.

SUMMITS
RED SCREES   2546ft/776m

START *Ambleside*   **Grid ref.** *NY 376045*

DISTANCE *7½ miles/12km*   **ASCENT** *2300ft/700m*

ORDNANCE SURVEY MAPS
1:50,000 - Landranger 90   1:25,000 - Outdoor Leisure 7

ACCESS *Start from the Market Place. There are several car parks. Served by bus from Windermere, Kendal and Keswick.*

Red Screes is a vast, whaleback mountain, and for seven of the ensuing miles the route is a mere ramble. The climb from Kirkstone to the summit, however, is a contrastingly steep haul with one or two rougher, more demanding moments.

S Leave the Market Place by the side road running past Barclays Bank onto a back road. This is Stock Ghyll Lane, signposted left behind the *Salutation Hotel* 'To the waterfalls'. Adjacent Stock Ghyll flows alongside, and when it parts company, be tempted to do likewise to experience the grandeur of Stock Ghyll Force. A path shadows the beck into the adjacent woodland of Stockghyll Park. When the path forks keep on the near side of the beck, climbing through the woods past several viewing stations for the spectacular cataracts. On gaining the top of the falls, turn right on a level path that doubles back to leave the wood at an antiquated turnstile.

Emerging back onto the lane, resume left, crossing a cattle-grid to emerge into the open, looking far up the valley of Stock Ghyll. Ahead, the great bulk of Red Screes overlooks the tiny dot of the *Kirkstone Pass Inn*, and this is a good opportunity to appraise virtually the whole walk. Our ascent line is the skyline ridge climbing from the pass beyond the south-east combe, with the long declining ridge to the left being the return route. Advance along a surfaced drive to Grove Farm.

Remain on the access road, passing the big house at Low Grove and rising to its demise at Grove Farm (Middle Grove on maps). At the far end a gate sees an inviting green track take up the running. This runs a delightful course as it traverses the flank of Wansfell, gaining height imperceptibly to approach the forlorn, tree-shrouded ruins of High Grove. Across the valley the sound of Pets Quarry can often be heard, producing traditional Lakeland green slate. The final stage beyond High Grove sees the way overlaid by a bulldozed eyesore of a track, which leads with some relief onto the Struggle, climbing from Ambleside to the summit of the Kirkstone Pass. Turn uphill to quickly gain the pub and A592 on the summit of the Kirkstone Pass.

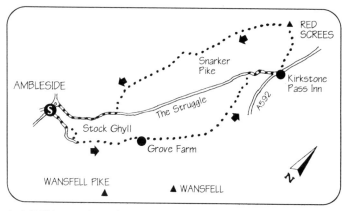

At 1492ft/455m the Kirkstone Pass is the highest road pass in Lakeland, and the only 'A' class one. Atop it stands the *Kirkstone Pass Inn*, one of the highest half-dozen pubs in the land and a possible purveyor of Dutch courage. Whether from its bar or just its door, it makes a good place from which to appraise the mountain's upper tiers. Countless car-borne visitors must have sat here and gazed in disbelief as walkers set forth to lay siege to this brooding mountain wall presenting its finest face for the benefit of non-walkers. A thousand feet of untamed fellside are no deterrent to those seeking the most expedient (if not the easiest!) route to any high mountain in the entire Lake District.

Turn immediately left into the car park, and leave by a kissing-gate at the far end. A path runs to the left over level ground before commencing the inevitable assault. The clear path winds pleasantly up through rocks to the base of the first craggy outcrops. Behind, Thornthwaite

Beacon appears above St. Raven's Edge. The path briefly splits, with a gentler left branch or a stony shoot to the right. The latter involves a minor scramble before they re-unite on the grass above. Look back now to see the long High Street skyline and the more shapely Ill Bell ridge having joined in.

At once a longer scree shoot is encountered. Either follow it or use grassy slopes to the left, where a gentler, spiralling path has formed for much of the way. Suddenly it alights onto a good path slanting up from the left. From this crossroads the easier way goes straight up, trending immediately left and working a clever route up between low out-crops. If turning right on the slanting path, this crosses the head of a scree gully and directly into another. Turn up this one, a rough clamber up partly loose rocks: it is easy enough with care, but would be less endearing if a clumsy party were higher up. During these strenuous efforts it will be readily clear as to how the mountain got its name! As the slopes relent escape out to the right and clamber up onto the grassy top. The easier path emerges some 60 or so yards over to the left, from where a path rises the short way to the waiting summit cairn.

Adorned by a large cairn, an Ordnance column, a shelter and a rather more decorative tarn, the highest point occupies an airy location atop a dramatic plunge to the Kirkstone road, where model cars appear to make laborious uphill progress. Glancing across at St. Raven's Edge on Caudale Moor, there is no indication of the deep trough of Kirkstone in between. Red Screes' relative isolation and clearly defined independence guarantee first-rate views, with ranges and groups to east and west, and distant lake scenery to north and south. Savour in particular the big view north as it is only available for the duration spent on the summit. Here Brotherswater and a glimpse of Ullswater are on offer, but the long return amble will be occupied by the long miles of Windermere.

Turn for home by beginning the long descent of Red Screes' south ridge. Initially heading left of the tarn, a good path forms to run on to a cairn above the brink of Raven Crag and the south-east combe, with another large cairn just beyond. The path continues down through the sparing contours of the ridge, a remarkable contrast after the latter stages of the ascent. Passing through a collapsed wall, a sturdier one then comes in from the left. These long strides offer ample opportunity to savour the grand array of mountains to the west.

The ridge narrows slightly to produce Snarker Pike (cairn over the wall), and from a well defined knoll Ambleside appears along with more of Windermere. The show is stolen, however, by the cameo of little Rydal Water nestling under colourful lower fells down to the right. Further down, the path is ushered down to the right by another wall, and from a stile begins a march down a green lane to end all green lanes. As height is lost the fells of the Fairfield Horseshoe increasingly dominate to the right, and the nearer, lower level scenery becomes increasingly attractive. In the fullness of time the green way emerges back onto the Struggle, and the final stretch leads down into the town. Near the bottom turn left down Fairview Road to continue down traffic-free Peggy Hill back into the centre.

Stock Ghyll Force

```
              SUMMITS
LITTLE HART CRAG   2090ft/637m
     DOVE CRAG   2598ft/792m
      HIGH PIKE   2152ft/656m
      LOW PIKE   1666ft/508m
```

START Ambleside   **Grid ref.** NY 376045

DISTANCE 10 miles/16km   **ASCENT** 2625ft/800m

ORDNANCE SURVEY MAPS
1:50,000 - Landranger 90   1:25,000 - Outdoor Leisure 7

ACCESS Start from the Market Place. Several car parks. Served by bus from Windermere, Kendal and Keswick.

A silent valley and a popular ridge make an excellent contrast on this walk which is far easier than its 10 miles suggest.

S From the market cross head along North Street, just above it, emerging onto Smithy Brow above the *Golden Rule*. Turn up a few yards, then go left along Sweden Bridge Lane. Remain on this to its narrowing end, where a gate signals the continuation as an enclosed cart track. Ahead are Low Pike and High Pike, our return ridge-route, then look round further left by way of Fairfield, Great Rigg, Heron Pike, Nab Scar, High Raise, the Langdale Pikes, Bowfell, the Coniston Fells, and the head of Windermere.

The track rises then swings pleasantly into woodland at the narrow neck of the valley of Scandale. Passing above tumbling waterfalls, the trees end as High Sweden Bridge is seen just ahead. This fine stone arched bridge is not crossed, but it makes a good first break spot. Resume upstream on the increasingly green track, which runs for the most part enclosed as Scandale Lane by broadly spaced walls into the sanctuary of Scandale. Ahead are the pairing of High Pike and Dove

Crag, the former, for now at least, misleadingly looking the most impressive. On a knoll, with the last stage of the dalehead in front, Little Hart Crag's twin summits appear on the skyline. All this fellwalk is now effectively on show.

Towards the end the path runs free, crossing the beck and running on to a gate just past a fine sheepfold complex. Here the climb to Scandale Pass begins, though climb is perhaps too grand a word for such an innocuous and quickly accomplished effort. A green path winds up through bracken then slants right to quickly level out on the summit of the pass. Up to the right are the spacious upper slopes of Red Screes, and the first view out of our hills, back down the valley to Coniston Old Man, is quickly joined by views ahead to the fells east of Patterdale.

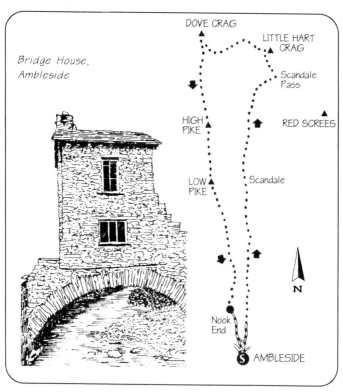

A stile in the watershed wall confirms arrival at the top of the pass. The twin peaks of Little Hart Crag are also waiting patiently, just above. Cross the stile and turn left up the path. At a wall corner a choice presents itself. The main branch goes left, passing above secretive Scandale Tarn, and after a general amble climbing to the prominent pillar on High Bakestones. Beyond that the path runs a few minutes further to join the main ridge descending south from Dove Crag.

For greater interest, take the path to the right with a line of old fenceposts. At once another branch offers itself, and this bears more to the right, bound for the fortress-like summit of Little Hart Crag. At its base another path is joined. Turn right for the couple of minutes climb to the neat summit. Bulky and lofty neighbours occupy much of the view to east and west, but the fell's position on the north-south watershed permits good views to the valley at Brotherswater one way, and down the length of Scandale's symmetrical bowl to Windermere the other. It also offers a good view of the sheer face of Dove Crag, the rockface which gives the day's major fell its name.

Retrace steps off the knoll, and resume on the main path which very quickly regains the fencepost path. This crosses the northern edge of Bakestones Moss above Black Brow, then shadows the fenceposts up steeper ground with Dove Crag's summit cairn appearing over to the right. This spell enjoys gorgeous views over Brotherswater and Hartsop. Path and posts run on for a level minute or two to join the main wallside path on the ridge, though in clear weather a short-cut can be made to the spacious summit, which stands a few yards east of the wall.

Here the celebrated round of the Fairfield Horseshoe is joined, a skyline circuit of Rydal Beck which means rather more fellow walkers are likely to be encountered from here-on. A rocky stance brightens up what is otherwise a featureless summit, for Dove Crag's pride and joy, its rockface overlooking Dovedale, seems in every sense a long way from this broad top. As a viewpoint, Dove Crag's highlight is the well proportioned skyline to the west between the Coniston and Buttermere fells.

Return by heading back south with the wall: now inextricably linked, path and wall cling to the watershed of this ridge which ends above Ambleside. Interruptions are encountered by the minor tops of High Pike and Low Pike. Though perhaps a worthwhile objective when doing the walk in reverse, the former is no more than a levelling out of the ridge, in descent. There is literally no re-ascent to its cairn which occupies a rocky crest above a profound drop into Scandale.

A steeper drop precedes the walk along to Low Pike, a far better beast which does at least demand a couple of minutes of re-ascent. Even then, the main path chooses to omit this by cutting round to its left. The top merits a visit however, and why question the wall-builders choice? Modest altitude and uninspiring name may conspire to do Low Pike less than justice, but it presents a distinctive outline from various locations in the Ambleside area. This shapely peak also provides a nice cameo of Rydal Water, while Bowfell looks particularly good amongst its peers over to the west.

Falling away sharply to the south, the ridge reveals a delightful view to the metropolis of Ambleside at the head of Windermere, which appears particularly extensive from close quarters. Continuing the descent the diversion quickly rejoins the main path, and a fork sends an alternative down to the left to resume on a lower, parallel line. The main path also forks, this being to avoid the Fairfield Horseshoe's very own 'Bad Step'. It is suddenly encountered on the wallside path, just as grassier and gentler paths through the bracken seem to be a fitting conclusion. This is no serious impasse, but it does demand a cautious approach and both hands out of pockets.

Beyond, ever easier going leads down to a gate just over to the left as the ridge wall is finally abandoned, and a firm track winds down to cross Scandale Beck on stone arched Low Sweden Bridge. Across it is Nook End Farm, from where simply follow narrow Nook Lane back into Ambleside.

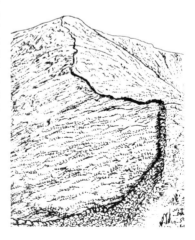

High Pike from Low Pike

27

SUMMITS
LOUGHRIGG FELL   1099ft/335m

START *White Moss Common* **Grid ref.** *NY 350065*

DISTANCE *4 miles/6½km*   **ASCENT** *1000ft/305m*

ORDNANCE SURVEY MAPS
1:50,000 - Landranger 90   1:25,000 - Outdoor Leisure 7

ACCESS *Start from the National Trust car park just below the A591 at the head of the lake, between Grasmere and Rydal. Ambleside-Grasmere-Keswick buses run past.*

Before starting it should be noted that this is an extremely popular location, drawing crowds in vast numbers, if only to the environs of the lakes and the lower slopes. Beware also of the extent of humble Loughrigg Fell, for its labyrinth of paths is quite unparalleled - you have been warned!

S From the car park take the broad path upstream with the initially unseen Rothay. Within five minutes a high footbridge is reached and the river is crossed. Immediately downstream, the river flows through a wetlands conservation area. Take the path heading directly away into Rydal Woods. It rises steadily to leave the trees at a gate, and here turn right up to a seat on a knoll. Both Rydal Water and Grasmere are in view, but it is the latter lake that is, for now, about to take centre-stage.

Just a few yards past the seat is a choice of continuing paths, opt for that rising steadily to the left. This is Loughrigg Terrace, a time-honoured favourite that traverses across Loughrigg's flank, gaining height only ever gently. Grasmere is now laid out delectably in its entirety below, and its beautiful vale is seen at its very best in the fullness of Autumn. Seats aplenty guarantee this section might take some time!

At the end of the terrace, do not go into the trees but turn up to the left to commence the climb proper. An initially steep path scales the fellside, evidence of its popularity being obvious in the extensively restored sections. When the going eases above the Grasmere cairn, a rise is topped and the summit appears just across a small depression.

The top is marked by an Ordnance column between small upthrusts of rock (see page 3), and is one of the few felltops regularly gained by the traditionally 'non-walking' motorist. Much of the surrounding valley scenery is obscured by Loughrigg's own sprawling flanks, but to the west the ground falls away sufficiently to reveal a glorious prospect of the Langdale valley, from shimmering Elterwater up to the dalehead protected by Bowfell and the inimitable Langdale Pikes. It is also at this point that the girth of this unique fell becomes apparent.

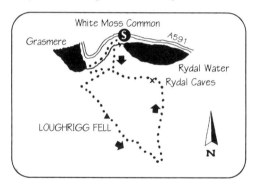

Resume the walk south-east in the direction of Windermere, on a clear path marked by large cairns. This drops to a distinct trough between scree-draped knolls. The main path's early steep section could be avoided by heading east from the summit, briefly, on another path which curves down to a small pool then down to the trough. The path quickly becomes a green swathe running on a broad shelf beneath the undulating ridge-line up to the left. When a wall briefly comes in on the right, avoid any branches left and keep on to drop to a distinct shelf with several attractive pools to the left. Just yards up to the right, at this point, a prominent cairned top offers a surprise view of Loughrigg Tarn.

The path continues gently down, slanting left on easy ground to reveal a broad, marshy depression seemingly far below. A fair portion of Loughrigg's extensive path network converges there, and the path drops more steeply to surprisingly quickly conclude with a steeper drop to its edge. Cross tiny Troughton Gill by a choice of paths (the right-hand one crosses at the main path junction, beneath a nearby pool). On the far bank a green path heads left, a short way above a thinner trod nearer the edge. Keeping the marshy tracts well to the left, the path rises steadily to a cairned brow. The path immediately begins an equally steady descent back towards Rydal Water, as yet unseen. Ahead, the Fairfield Horseshoe is well presented.

An inviting minor top to the right may encourage a detour, while over to the left, the folds and tors of Loughrigg's higher slopes suggest a far greater altitude for this fell. Descending through a slender juniper zone, tranquil Rydal Water at last appears along with white-walled Nab Cottage. Rising behind is the increasingly dominant rough face of Nab Scar. Eventually the path comes down to meet a broad track at a stone bridge. Turning left it rises immediately to one of Loughrigg's enormous caves, mute memorials to slate quarrying days.

Just beyond the cave the track winds up to a larger yawning hole. This is more easily accessible and invites a paddle into its darker recesses: giant stepping-stones afford even easier entry. A minute or so beyond the cave the path forks at a seat. Opt for the near-level upper one, which runs above a plantation. When it forks bear right, and at the next fork, there are two choices. For the direct finish bear right again to the gate into Rydal Woods, and retrace initial steps back to the start.

If keen to continue, keep straight on at the second fork to reach the walk's first seat above the woods. This time take the path below Loughrigg Terrace, slanting down to the prominent upper footbridge just below the outflow from Grasmere. Downstream paths on either bank then lead back to the first footbridge, and thus the start point.

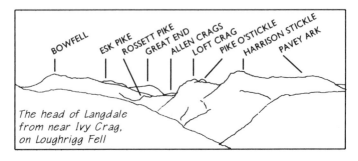

BOWFELL ESK PIKE ROSSETT PIKE GREAT END ALLEN CRAGS LOFT CRAG PIKE O'STICKLE HARRISON STICKLE PAVEY ARK

The head of Langdale
from near Ivy Crag,
on Loughrigg Fell

```
                SUMMITS
STONE ARTHUR   1652ft/504m
  GREAT RIGG   2513ft/766m
   FAIRFIELD   2864ft/873m
```

START Grasmere   **Grid ref.** NY 337076

DISTANCE 8½ miles/13½km   **ASCENT** 2900ft/884m

ORDNANCE SURVEY MAPS
1:50,000 - Landranger 90
1:25,000 - Outdoor Leisure 5, Outdoor Leisure 7

ACCESS Start from the green in the village centre. There are large car parks nearby. Served by Ambleside-Keswick buses.

Fairfield is the major top in a neatly defined group south of Helvellyn, and this outing will offer much interest whilst avoiding the bulk of the crowds undertaking the celebrated 'Horseshoe' walk, from Ambleside.

S From the bookshop corner on the green, follow the main road (Swan Lane) up to the A591. Cross to the *Swan Hotel* and head straight off along the back road alongside it. As the road swings round to the left take an access road on the right, signed to Greenhead Gill and Alcock Tarn. This climbs in the company of the beck to terminate before a gate onto the base of the fell. Here turn left above the intake wall, a good path rising outside a plantation. Remain with this to climb steeply, then bear left to the top end of the trees.

At a wall junction here the path turns sharp right and rises more gently. Stone Arthur's knobbly top is in view ahead now. The path runs on to a stream crossing between old walls almost lost in the bracken. It then traverses to the right, slanting in a large loop up to the top wall corner, still deep in bracken. The wall leads briefly left before the path resumes its climb. By now the crag-defended summit waits just ahead.

Escaping the bracken the path rises through the ultimately innocuous obstructions of the upper slopes to claim the 'top' of Stone Arthur. In truth the top is hard to define, as this is merely the craggy spur of a broad ridge descending from Great Rigg. However, advantage should be taken of one of the many upthrusts of rock for a natural seat complete with backrest, to savour the picture of Grasmere's sheet of water in its green vale enclosed by colourful fells.

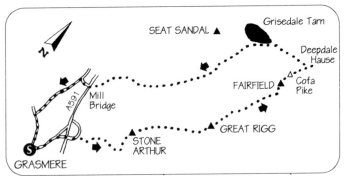

Resume on the clear path beginning a long, gentle and enjoyable rise to Great Rigg. Towards the top a lengthy section of Windermere appears over Heron Pike to the right, and the path then joins the ridge-top Fairfield Horseshoe path. Turn left for a short, stony climb to the strapping cairn on Great Rigg. A prized feature of its view is the exceptional amount of water to be seen, not merely in the number of tarns, but also the sheer extent of the larger lakes, Windermere and Coniston Water. Descent is minimal before a prolonged and very easy rise onto Fairfield. In the final stages the path becomes fainter on the broad, stony top, and in unfavourable conditions caution is needed in finding the main summit cairn (incorporating a shelter) before the steep eastern plunge.

As a viewpoint Fairfield ranks highly, with an unbroken western skyline beyond miles of lower ground; a striking line-up of the Helvellyn range from a satisfying angle; and an extensive picture of the High Street group. A perambulation of the summit plateau is repaid with a much improved view to the north, where Cofa Pike is revealed on the ridge descending to Deepdale Hause. As this is the point of departure, locate an improving path descending stony slopes to Cofa Pike's rugged little peak.

The crossing of this bristly eminence demands a steady hold for a few yards if traversing its true crest. Enjoying fine views into the bowl of Grisedale Tarn and down Grisedale and Deepdale, the path resumes steeply and enjoyably down through minor outcrops to Deepdale Hause. Advance to the far end, and as the ridge prepares to climb to Saint Sunday Crag, a cairn marks a path doubling back left. This fine mountain path slants down to cross to the foot of Grisedale Tarn.

The sizeable tarn is overlooked by sombre slopes which though largely turning their backs, nevertheless provide a splendid mountain atmosphere. Ahead are Dollywaggon Pike's unrelenting flanks, while to its left stands Seat Sandal. Looking back to the right, Saint Sunday Crag asserts itself gracefully above Grisedale. Resume by taking the broad path branching left just before the outflow of the tarn, to face the last uphill section. This steady slant leads back across Fairfield's flank to the summit of Grisedale Hause at 1935ft/590m.

Turning through the pass, the part pitched path descends into the amphitheatre of Hause Moss, then runs on to commence the long descent to Grasmere, whose green vale unfolds below. After passing a pair of massive boulders the only steep section of the descent is encountered, in the process crossing Tongue Gill below an attractive waterfall. The going soon eases and a steady march down the slope gives time to fully savour the view ahead.

Towards the end the path slants down to a small reservoir, then down to a footbridge on Tongue Gill. Just across it Little Tongue Gill is also crossed to a gate off the fell, by a sheepfold. A broad, enclosed track runs down high above the beck, emerging back onto the A591 at Mill Bridge. Cross straight over and down the back road to Low Mill Bridge, keeping left at succeeding junctions to enter the village on Easedale Road.

The northern peaks and ridges of the Coniston Fells, from the upper reaches of Tongue Gill

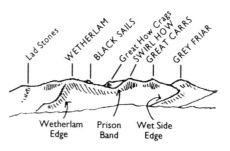

```
              SUMMITS
   SEAT SANDAL    2415ft/736m
```

START Grasmere   **Grid ref.** NY 336091

DISTANCE 5½ miles/9km   **ASCENT** 2265ft/690m

ORDNANCE SURVEY MAPS
1:50,000 - Landranger 90
1:25,000 - Outdoor Leisure 5

ACCESS Start from the A591 at Mill Bridge, a long half-mile north of the Swan Hotel. There are useful lay-bys either side of the bend here. Windermere-Grasmere-Keswick bus service.

An independent fell with a distinct outline in the heart of the district, Seat Sandal nevertheless attracts few walkers. It is a permanent feature in the Grasmere scene, but struggles for attention in the face of more appealing, lower heights such as Silver How and Helm Crag.

S At Mill Bridge cross to the cluster of dwellings on the east side of the road, from where a time-honoured track is faithfully signposted to Patterdale. Heading up past the houses it climbs steeply above Tongue Gill to gain the base of the fell at a gate by a sheepfold. Here cross Little Tongue Gill and then a footbridge on Tongue Gill itself. The path rises past a small reservoir to commence a steady pull across the flanks of the Fairfield group, rising effortlessly until a steeper, repaired section climbs to cross the main stream at a lovely waterfall. The climb continues but soon eases out to enter the amphitheatre of Hause Moss, with the top of Grisedale Hause just ahead now. One final short pull gains the crest of the pass at 1935ft/590m.

Revealed below in its bowl of fells is Grisedale Tarn, whose outflow is the objective of the main path. For Seat Sandal, however, turn sharp left on the path climbing with the old wall. This short, roughish pull quickly eases out to run gently on to the summit cairn. Seat Sandal's two main pluses as a viewpoint are the numerous sheets of water in sight (and sizeable portions, to boot), and the uninterrupted panorama to the west across the lower gulf of central fells beyond Dunmail Raise.

Leave by heading due north, the faint wall returning within a few yards of the summit cairn, and leading the way unfailingly down grassy slopes to the broad saddle with the imposing bulk of Dollywaggon Pike, straight ahead. At the path junction on the saddle turn right, running along the base of Dollywaggon Pike, with the tarn on the right. At the end of the tarn the main path prepares to descend into Grisedale, so turn right on a path to the outflow. This extensive sheet of water is overlooked by sombre fells, which though largely turning their backs nevertheless provide a splendid mountain atmosphere. To the right are the rough slopes of Fairfield, but pride of place goes to the graceful peak of Saint Sunday Crag overlooking Grisedale. Interestingly for its size, the tarn has virtually no inflowing streams.

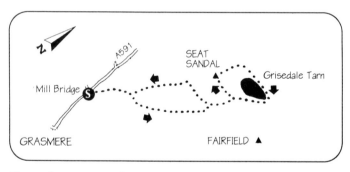

The outflowing stream being easily crossed, a path rises gently across Fairfield's flank back onto Grisedale Hause. A splendid alternative to the outward path is available: commencing the long steady return to Grasmere, retrace steps down past Hause Moss, reaching a cairn just beyond a pair of massive boulders. As the only steep section looms, leave the outward path where this cairn sends the original, less used bridle track off to the right, initially as a much thinner path. This contours above a line of low crags on the flanks of Seat Sandal before turning to enjoy a super descent through the bracken of Little Tongue. Ahead, the charms of Grasmere's green vale unfold. Lower down the path runs as a well engineered green way in the company of Little Tongue Gill, meeting the main path at the base of the open fell, to retrace opening steps back to the road.

SILVER HOW

SUMMITS	
SILVER HOW	*1296ft/395m*

START *Grasmere* **Grid ref.** *NY 337076*

DISTANCE *3½ miles/5½km* **ASCENT** *1100ft/335m*

ORDNANCE SURVEY MAPS
1:50,000 - Landranger 90 *1:25,000 - Outdoor Leisure 7*

ACCESS *Start from the green in the village centre. Large car parks nearby. Served by Windermere-Ambleside-Keswick buses.*

Few would decry Silver How's claim to be the loveliest of Lakeland's lower fells, and by the time this walk is over it will have yet more fans.

S From the green cross to the left of the Heaton Cooper gallery, where a cul-de-sac lane leaves a crossroads by the adjacent cafe. At once, our inviting objective rises to the left. Within a couple of minutes the lane transforms into a parkland drive. Approaching Allan Bank (one of Wordsworth's former homes), stay on the drive bearing round to the right and continue uphill to its demise at an enviably sited farm. Already, there are delightful views over the Vale of Grasmere, from the Helm Crag ridge round to Seat Sandal and Fairfield.

From a gate to the left of the farm a path rises away, soon becoming enclosed. It climbs onto the open fell to undertake an undemanding if steep pull up by the wall. Grasmere's lake appears down to the left, though it will soon be better seen. The path continues more gently as a fine green way through dense juniper. Shortly before escaping these bushes the main path bears left to a knoll, then on a few yards further to approach Wray Gill. Turn upstream for less than a hundred yards before crossing the briefly tamed ravine in colourful surroundings. The path climbs gentler slopes opposite, and before reaching a substantial cairn the summit appears ahead. Only the final climb brings any steepness to this upper half of the ascent, which is further enlivened by an improving prospect to the right of the Langdale Pikes.

Fells on view to the south and the west include Wetherlam, Swirl How, Great Carrs, Pike o'Blisco, Crinkle Crags, Bowfell, Langdale Pikes, and Sergeant Man. Remarkably, this stunning array of hills is equalled by a glorious prospect of lakes and valleys, featuring Grasmere and Rydal Water in virtual entirety, also Windermere, Loughrigg Tarn and Elterwater.

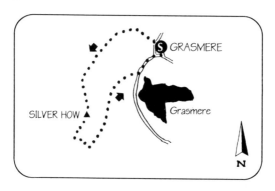

On leaving the summit cairn head south, a sketchy path materialising to aim for a large, prominent cairn a short quarter-mile distant. Once at the cairn continue a little further, dropping down to locate a substantial cairn on a knoll down to the left. A thin, level path is joined to lead down to it. A clearer path now drops down to a scrappy cairn at a crossroads of paths on the extensive level ground below. The path heading left is the return route, although a brief foray to the right will bring an improved and final view into Great Langdale, the ground falling away dramatically as Meg's Gill above the environs of Chapel Stile.

The return to Grasmere calls for little description, the path being clear throughout and giving ample opportunity to appraise Grasmere's lake in its green vale. The descent is everywhere well graded, initially through zones of juniper. A wall comes in for company beneath Silver How's steep flanks, but little else changes. The wall ultimately ushers the path down to a kissing-gate, then it winds down through two varied pastures before becoming enclosed to quickly debouch onto the Red Bank road opposite the boat landings. All that remains is a short walk to the left back into the village.

```
SUMMITS
HELM CRAG    1328ft/405m
GIBSON KNOTT   1384ft/422m
CALF CRAG   1761ft/537m
```

START Grasmere   **Grid ref.** NY 337076

DISTANCE 8 miles/13km   **ASCENT** 2000ft/610m

ORDNANCE SURVEY MAPS
1:50,000 - Landranger 90
1:25,000 - Outdoor Leisure 6, Outdoor Leisure 7

ACCESS Start from the green in the village centre. There are large car parks nearby, and a small one on Easedale Road (actually on the walk) which saves a little distance but is soon full. Served by Ambleside-Keswick buses.

The Grasmere scene would be robbed of an important element without the familiar outline of Helm Crag, a landmark known far beyond fellwalkers' circles.

⑤ Leave the green along Easedale Road, which sets off from the bookshop corner in the direction of the youth hostels. Keeping doggedly on, a section before Goody Bridge offers a parallel footway. The road shortly enters green pastures, only losing its solid surface at the small collection of desirable properties across the field. The continuing rough track turns up to the right, past the last house to gain the base of Helm Crag's steep slopes. Just a few yards further a fork is reached and the climbing can commence.

The path to the right sets off on a winding course that follows an initially heavily restored line up Helm Crag's flank, avoiding the first few hundred feet of the old path that is being left to recover from erosion. Just before it is rejoined on the ridge-end, with its anticipated view down into the Vale of Grasmere, a pause to look ahead up the valley of Far Easedale will reveal the whole route, including the two other tops to be visited. Once on the ridge-end only a short but lively clamber up through the outcrops remains before the summit ridge is gained.

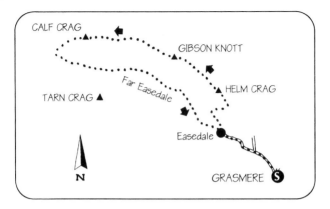

There can be no other felltop quite like Helm Crag, for this is a bewildering wonderland that demands careful exploration. The summit is a long spine, a double ridge with a low trough running between. The highest point is found at the far end of the short ridge, where a tilted tower of rock points skyward. Known by various names, best as the Howitzer, what is certain is that an adventurous scramble is required to claim to have gained the fell's true summit. Helm Crag is better known to tourists as the Lion and the Lamb, and it is the grouping of rocks first encountered that usually give rise to this title. From here the Vale of Grasmere is seen as on a map, a verdant scene that typifies Lakeland, while toy cars race over Dunmail Raise, occupants craning their necks to our lofty perch.

Next top along this ridge dividing Far Easedale and Greenburn is Gibson Knott, and the way thereto is straightforward. A cairn just beyond the rock tower signals the start of a short but rough descent, from where a much gentler pull leads onto Gibson Knott. The main path in fact cheats on the ridge proper, and outflanks several outcrops by traversing the Far Easedale flank below the skyline. Two cairns adorn the top, the lower one being rather a better viewpoint: a particular feast for the eyes is the intimidating rock-bound flank of Tarn Crag across the gulf formed by the head of Far Easedale.

The path continues unfailingly westward towards Calf Crag, but again exhibits a preference for the Far Easedale side of the ridge and avoids one or two more sporting opportunities. After gentle ambling it climbs a little past Pike of Carrs, a prominent feature from the valley, then encounters an unappealing marshy plateau before the final section to the summit. Thankfully this is a grand spot to struggle to, for the neat cairn sits amidst outcrops above a steep fall to the valley. This is also the place for which to save the sandwiches, far from the throngs venturing only as far as the Lion and the Lamb.

Although the overlord of its ridge, Calf Crag's top is only minutes from the pass connecting it with the bigger fells to which it really belongs. From the summit the path continues on to drop only a short way to the head of Far Easedale. Here a stile offers assistance to the short sighted, but visitors may be more puzzled by this 'pass that isn't'. A busy thoroughfare through the hills links Borrowdale and Grasmere, but this saddle is only the lower of two that the route uses, the main one being the pass of Greenup Edge beyond the head of Wythburn.

Whatever its status it is good enough for us, so turn left to commence an infallible return to Grasmere. The path soon crosses to the south bank of Far Easedale Gill above some falls, until well down the valley where it returns to the other side. Here, Stythwaite Steps have been rendered redundant by a basic footbridge. The path now broadens into a stony track, initially in the company of the beck, to return to the houses of Easedale, to then retrace steps back to the village.

*Summit rocks,
Helm Crag*

SUMMITS	
STEEL FELL	1814ft/553m

START Grasmere   **Grid ref.** NY 331095

DISTANCE 4½ miles/7km   **ASCENT** 1540ft/470m

ORDNANCE SURVEY MAPS
1:50,000 - Landranger 90
1:25,000 - Outdoor Leisure 5

ACCESS Start from Gill Foot, off the A591 at the foot of Dunmail Raise, beneath Town Head. Roadside parking on the verge east of the bridge. The A591 is served by Windermere-Ambleside-Keswick buses.

Steel Fell is an unsung hill in the heart of the district, offering a fascinating walk far from the crowds.

S Cross the bridge and take the private drive climbing steeply right. Ahead looms the final stage of the walk, the descent from Steel Fell, while across to the right is the farming hamlet of Town Head, with one of its white-walled cottages sporting distinctive round chimneys. Past two cottages at the top, the drive ends at a gate. The Greenburn Valley awaits, and a splendid path runs along the wallside. Up to the left the weird summit rocks of Helm Crag catch the eye, as they will do for much of the early and final stages.

The path runs on to rise beneath a rocky bluff in the company of the Green Burn. As it rounds the knoll the excellent workmanship of this old green way is revealed, its retaining wall still serving its purpose as well as ever. The track runs on above a small dam on the beck, then rises ever gently before a sudden arrival in Greenburn Bottom. This is a splendid moment as the dead-flat, marshy amphitheatre is gained, an unassuming sanctuary in the hills. Even to the untrained eye, the drumlins (rounded heaps of glacial moraine) are very evident around the perimeter of this hollow.

The path crosses the outflow on a collection of stepping-stones, and resumes as a superlative green way up the side of the valley. Ahead, the great bulk of Ullscarf overtops our own walk's skyline. A sheepfold is passed employing two massive boulders as corner-stones, and the way rises ever gently across the lower flanks of Gibson Knott. Across the moist basin runs the long skyline ridgewalk to Steel Fell's summit. At a cairn on a green knoll the path forks, the main path (not ours) climbing left to join the Calf Crag-Gibson Knott ridge just above.

Our escape from the valley is to be by way of the very dalehead, where the stream issues forth at the very headwall. Forging straight on, therefore, the way fades by the time a massive boulder thatched with heather is reached. From here there are two ways of gaining the objective. Easiest option is to angle gently down towards the foot of the falling beck, then rise steadily and pleasantly on the grassy slopes on its near side (omit the next paragraph to pick up the route).

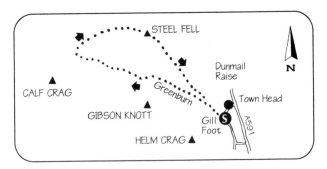

Alternatively, forge on from the boulder and rise very gently, ideally to latch onto a faint grassy rake. This involves traversing above the isolated outcrop beneath the higher Rough Crag, and tracing this old way at a uniform slant across the fell to reach the well defined course of a side gill. Just across the other bank is the objective of this long abandoned path, a ruined sheepfold on a knoll beneath a rocky tor. From the fold slant up beneath the outcrop onto easier ground above the lower route, and curve round to approach the main stream.

At the easing out of the main stream and its slopes, cross the tiny beck and double back up to the right across easy ground to pick up the watershed path and fenceposts. Seemingly very much in the back of beyond, it is interesting to consider that we are in fact in the heart of

Lakeland. Turn right along the ridge-path, past a sizeable pool with Ullscarf behind. The path weaves in and out of the old fenceposts, a pleasant roller-coaster which runs on to meet a fence corner. Here Thirlmere appears in a big way down to the left, with the ever-imposing Helvellyn range rising behind: nearer to hand, note also the impressive face of Nab Crags on Ullscarf's flank. The fence leads quickly up and along to the summit cairn.

The panorama offers plenty of interest, though most of the features on offer are better seen at other stages of the walk. Given the extensive nature of the top, the view of Thirlmere is surprisingly good. Leave by the thin path heading south-east, briefly down gentle ground before reaching a steeper drop. The A591's long climb to Dunmail Raise appears far below, quickly joined by the south-east ridge, a simple and obvious line of descent. The clearer path winds down this briefly steep section before a steady decline, encountering a couple more halts before running down through bracken to a wall. Through the gate the path resumes through several pastures, and from the gate at the bottom corner descends as a fine green way through bracken. It slants down to meet the outward route at the entrance to Greenburn. Return through the gate and back down the drive to finish.

Steel Fell reflected in Thirlmere, from the north

```
              SUMMITS
   TARN CRAG    1807ft/551m
```

START Grasmere   **Grid ref.** NY 337076

DISTANCE 7 miles/11km   **ASCENT** 1575ft/480m

ORDNANCE SURVEY MAPS
1:50,000 - Landranger 90
1:25,000 - Outdoor Leisure 6, Outdoor Leisure 7

ACCESS Start from the green in the village centre. There are large car parks nearby, and a small one on Easedale Road (actually on the walk) which saves a little distance but is soon full. Served by Ambleside-Keswick buses.

Occupying an enviable position in central Lakeland, Tarn Crag nevertheless remains relatively little known, yet its only failing is a lack of independence. Behind its facade higher ground rises almost immediately to continue to High Raise, a disappointment of little consequence on this ascent of the east ridge, a pre-eminent way to the summit.

S Leave the green by Easedale Road, which departs in the direction of the youth hostels from the bookshop corner. En route to Goody Bridge it offers an adjacent footway; at the road junction here, keep straight on, the road shortly crossing a field to the small group of dwellings of Far Easedale. Pass to the right between the houses to a gate onto the base of Helm Crag. Keeping left, a rough track runs along the valley floor. To the left, Blea Rigg rises behind Brimmer Head Farm, while ahead is Tarn Crag with the continuing slopes of High Raise behind.

Part way on, Far Easedale Gill is joined for a lovely stroll to reach a basic wooden footbridge alongside the stepping-stones at Stythwaite Steps. Only a hundred yards after crossing, the valley path is forsaken for an improving path forking left to climb parallel with a wall. As the wall departs past a heather bedecked boulder, the path continues up to quickly gain the broad ridge descending from Tarn Crag.

Ahead, across a small marshy tract, is the well blazed path leaving the top of Sourmilk Gill for Easedale Tarn, with the craggy wall of Blea Rigg rising behind. Saving that for the return journey, our route forks in the rampant bracken of the ridge, and a distinct green path swings up to the right. At once - though it will playfully disappear at random - the summit appears, being the sharp peak to the right of the rounded dome. All is now plain sailing as the path gains height in delightful fashion, soon escaping the choking bracken to climb to a prominent knoll. During this stage one can regularly watch the crowds walking up to Easedale Tarn. At this knoll the tarn itself makes its first appearance in dramatic style, while a permanent feature across to the right is the Helm Crag-Calf Crag ridge backed by the Helvellyn skyline.

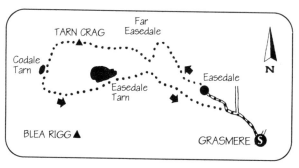

Occasionally the path inexplicably fades on steeper sections, but its course remains obvious to arrive at a grassy saddle prior to the final steeper pull through more interesting rocky terrain. Worth noting here are the great wall of Deer Bield Crags on the fell's northern flank, and the appearance of the higher feet of Harrison Stickle and Pavey Ark fronting the Langdale Pikes. A few yards' stroll to the left, meanwhile, reveals a wonderful prospect over the tarn, again. Note also a path descending from this point to the tarn's shore, should the need arise.

A little higher, as the now close to hand craggy summit beckons, a clever zigzag path climbs left to sneak up through a pronounced gap in the craggy slopes. At the top the path continues on, but the summit cairn is found by a climb of only a few feet up to the right. Level ground runs behind for some distance before it re-ascends colourful sprawling slopes towards High Raise.

A neat cairn perches on a rocky promontory, an exquisite spot for a sojourn to take in the outstandingly beautiful view of Easedale and Grasmere. The lack of Easedale Tarn in the view can be remedied by making for the large cairn across the path, then as this fails to deliver the goods, moving a few yards further to the rim of the crags. This straying from the path is not recommended in bad visibility. Also in view, waterwise, are Windermere, Grasmere and Rydal Water, while the elusive Codale Tarn sits in a hollow to the south-west, backed by the ever shapely Langdale Pikes.

Codale Tarn is also the key to the descent, though a bee-line is not the best way: instead return to the path running on from the ascent. It soon skirts the right side of a marsh, and then, faced with small outcrops the path begins to climb. Here take a slender fork towards a knoll over to the left. Within 30 yards, before reaching the knoll, Codale Tarn appears below. An improving path drops down the steeper slope to the right, with a ruinous sheepfold further to the right.

Bound directly for the tarn, the latter stage crosses a plateau to arrive at its shore. This is very much a tranquil spot to linger, and much to be preferred to the more populous shoreline of Easedale Tarn soon to be reached. Again improved, the path runs along the tarn's modest length, crossing its tiny outflow as it goes. Continuing on around the grassy rear of Belles Knott, the path curves down to join the much trodden path descending to the outspread Easedale Tarn from the Sergeant Man ridge.

Turn down the path's initially stony course before it runs on through partly marshy environs to the outlet of Easedale Tarn. This popular objective of the casual walker is yet another place to linger. The path turns down from the tarn foot and crosses another marshy hollow before a steeper but enjoyable drop alongside the effervescent tumble of Sourmilk Gill. At the foot of the fell it runs along through several pastures interrupted by a spell with the beck to reach the restored New Bridge. Keep on the broad path to cross a small footbridge enshrouded in trees, before emerging back onto the Easedale Road near the start of the walk.

SUMMITS
BLEA RIGG   1775ft/541m

START Grasmere   **Grid ref.** NY 337076

DISTANCE 7½ miles/12km   **ASCENT** 1800ft/550m

ORDNANCE SURVEY MAPS
1:50,000 - Landranger 90
1:25,000 - Outdoor Leisure 6, Outdoor Leisure 7

ACCESS Start from the green in the village centre. Large car parks nearby. Served by Windermere-Ambleside-Keswick buses.

Blea Rigg divides beautiful Grasmere from incomparable Langdale, and while it is in truth a bulky ridge rather than a seperate fell, it still conjures up a summit to crown an already superb outing.

S Leave the green by Easedale Road, which departs in the direction of the youth hostels from the bookshop corner. En route to Goody Bridge it offers an adjacent footway; at the road junction here, keep straight on. Just prior to the road entering a field, take a footbridge on Easedale Beck in the trees on the left. Ahead, the cataracts of Sourmilk Gill beckon the wide and popular path. It runs through several pastures interrupted by a spell with the beck alongside the rebuilt New Bridge. Soon the path gains the base of the fell to commence a climb that revels in the spectacular water features of Sourmilk Gill. At the top of the waterfalls the gradients ease for a steady stroll up to the foot of Easedale Tarn, a favourite objective of William Wordsworth.

Across the tarn towers Tarn Crag, while up to the left are the savagely rough walls of Blea Crag. Remain on the path along the left bank of the tarn, part marshy and part rebuilt until it commences a more serious climb between Eagle Crag on Blea Rigg, and the temporarily magnificent pyramid of Belles Knott - Wainwright's 'Matterhorn of Easedale'. Rough and stony, the path improves a little above Belles

Knott to slant up the colourful slopes. Secretive Codale Tarn is revealed behind Belles Knott, joining the prospect of the lower level Easedale Tarn. At the top the climb steepens to emerge amid numerous cairns onto the ridge falling from Sergeant Man to Blea Rigg.

The multiplicity of cairns and pathways on the ridge-top need not cause confusion. Ignoring the main path slanting up to the right, bound for Sergeant Man, advance for a couple of minutes across the gentle slope to gain the true crest of this broad ridge, and a good path will be found. We are now in the bizarre situation of attaining the highest point of the walk before reaching our summit, due to Blea Rigg being only a minor interruption on the great, reluctantly declining ridge. These thoughts are soon put behind as the magnificent prospect of Harrison Stickle and Pavey Ark's upper slopes appears ahead.

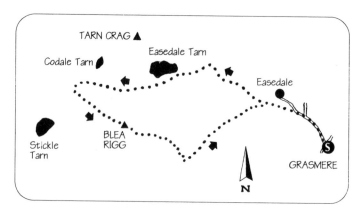

Turning left on the path, Windermere is seen distantly ahead, while early on there is a brief glimpse back to the right of the shimmering waters of Stickle Tarn below Harrison Stickle. The path quickly undertakes a modest descent onto a plateau, and skirts to the left of a pair of rocky knolls. Some exhilarating views are enjoyed down to Easedale and Codale Tarns, but be aware that the abrupt wall of Blea Crag hovers just a short distance below the path.

The path meanders on to locate the accepted summit towards the end of the higher part of the ridge. It is set back some 50 yards up to the right, and clearly few walkers bother to make the detour. A decent cairn sits on a rock tor, and though there appears to be higher ground across the depression to the west, this deserves the status of arbitrary summit: certainly there is nothing resembling higher ground beyond this point. The attractive view includes a fair prospect of the floor of Langdale, featuring Elterwater, otherwise rarely visible from this broad ridge. Also on parade are the Coniston Fells, Pike o'Blisco, Crinkle Crags, and still of course the Langdale Pikes. More distantly, beyond Windermere, a clear day reveals the Howgill Fells and Ingleborough, in the Pennines.

Immediately below the summit the main path swings right, directly under the top, and enjoys a steeper descent. A plateau of pools and marshes precedes a crossing of the knolls of Great Castle How. Dropping to another marshy basin, cross the outflow on its left and over the final knoll of Little Castle How. The basin of Blindtarn Moss is partially visible far below, with our intended path out of it clearly in view as it heads into the bracken. The present path now slants down beneath an old roofed shelter into the marsh of Swinescar Hause. One final glance up Langdale will reveal Bowfell has now joined Crinkle Crags.

Vacate the path near the foot of the drop as it undertakes a wide sweep around the marsh. If wishing to remain on the ridge, incidentally, the continuation to Silver How is easily accomplished. The descent route, meanwhile, drops down to the left to cross the narrow neck of the marsh, from where an initially sketchy path sets off down to the left, indicated by a small cairn on a rock. It becomes clear as the ground steepens for the descent into the seldom visited bowl of Blindtarn Moss. The valley floor of Easedale is seen beyond. Though sometimes sketchy further down, occasional cairns serve to confirm what is a generally obvious course through rampant juniper into this colourful hollow.

Crossing the side of the moss an improved path takes shape in the bracken, the intense greenery proving a little claustrophobic in late summer. Easedale appears much closer below now, and Blindtarn Gill puts in an appearance as the path winds down past the walled enclosure of Great Intake to the rear of a lone dwelling. Through the gate to its right the drive is followed away, and as the track turns off, keep straight on beside a small wood. A minor bank in the next field leads to a gate back onto the outward path on the valley floor. Turning right, the road and thence Grasmere are soon reached.

SUMMITS
PAVEY ARK   2296ft/700m
HARRISON STICKLE   2415ft/736m
PIKE O'STICKLE   2326ft/709m
LOFT CRAG   2231ft/680m

START Dungeon Ghyll   **Grid ref.** NY 295064

DISTANCE 4 miles/6½km   **ASCENT** 2510ft/765m

ORDNANCE SURVEY MAPS
1:50,000 - Landranger 89 **or** 90   1:25,000 - Outdoor Leisure 6

ACCESS Start from the New Hotel, half a mile short of the B5343's end at the Old Hotel. There are National Park and National Trust car parks. Served by bus from Ambleside.

Nowhere in Britain is a walk's distance as irrelevant a measure of its content as on the Cuillin of Skye, and though on an admittedly smaller scale, don't scorn this outing on account of its humble mileage. Although an easier option exists, the purpose of this walk is to gain the Langdale summits by the finest possible route, the scramble up Jack's Rake high above Stickle Tarn.

S From the drive to the hotel and its hamlet, go straight on through a gate by the side of a cottage. Head up the wallside to a gateway and into an enclosure behind, where the path from the NT car park comes in. Rise between small clusters of trees and remain on the restored path by Stickle Gill. The lively beck is soon crossed at a sturdy footbridge. Resume upstream, initially steadily before the path climbs unrelentingly and enjoyably, inviting minor scrambles over streamside rocks. Ultimately the crest of Pavey Ark peers over the lip of the combe, and then that's it, the classic moment as Pavey Ark's mighty cliff looms across the waters of Stickle Tarn; an experience that never diminishes with repetition. The surviving dam was made to enlarge the tarn and ensure a water supply for gunpowder works at Elterwater.

Now is the time to appraise the upper half of the ascent. More a cliff face than a fell, no crag is better known by the fellwalker than Pavey Ark, for instead of simply gazing at it, he can if moderately agile expect to make his way up the centre of it. The grounds for this accessibility is Jack's Rake, a line of weakness that crosses the face from bottom right to top left. Though clearly discernible, the probability of it being a walkers' route seems decidedly unlikely. Those overwhelmed by the prospect can opt to omit Pavey Ark entirely, and instead climb between the crag and Harrison Stickle to the left.

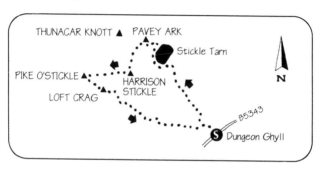

Whilst either side of the tarn can be followed to access the start of the scramble, the more commonly used route crosses the outflow and goes left before slanting up the scree to the foot of the cliff. The Rake starts at the very base of the biggest buttress. At the same point, aptly named Easy Gully offers an alternative route.

Once embarked upon, the route of Jack's Rake is difficult to lose: the direction and the angle change little, and certainly there is little else to deflect you. For the most part this simple scramble is protected from the anticipated sense of exposure by a low rock wall which confines the often wet gully. Only near the top does this defensive wall falter, and even then only mild caution is needed to offset any possibility of mishaps. At the top, swing up to the right for a short clamber over boulders to the summit cairn. Savour this moment, there are few adventures such as this for the humble fellwalker.

Leave by a path heading 'inland', almost at once crossing an old wall and then curving left, bound for Harrison Stickle. A dependable series of cairns guide this enjoyable path across a veritable boulderfield. As the terrain eases the path swings round to the right alongside a couple of pools, and picking up a path coming down off Thunacar Knott, skirts the right side of a rock tor to reach a high saddle under the summit crown of Harrison Stickle. A five minute clamber will have the highest point underfoot. The summit lives up to the fell's general appeal, a bristly crown bedecked with shapely cairns. To south and east crags guard the top, and from here the most dramatic views are obtained. Three distinctly different features earn a mention, the first being an aerial view of Langdale, its lush, green floor curving away towards Windermere; second is a side-on picture of Pavey Ark hovering above Stickle Tarn; and third an outstanding line-up of lofty peaks hemming in the dalehead.

Most inviting aspect for us is shapely Pike o'Stickle. Retrace steps to the minor saddle between the summit and the small rock tor to the north. At a junction here take the left branch, descending easy ground to meet another path just short of the stream in the amphitheatre of Harrison Combe. Cross over the stream and remain on the path bound directly for Pike o'Stickle. The path rises to the head of the great scree shoot where Neolithic man had stone axe 'factories'. The scree run was at one time a Lakeland classic, ensuring a rapid return to the valley for those confident on its sliding stones. Unfortunately they've all slid now, and it is firmly not recommended as a descent route.

Pike o'Stickle's graceful cone thrusts itself skyward from the mass of the mountainside and the barricade of cliffs wrapped around it, and the final climb is as exhilarating as one cares to make it: the normal route climbs to the right before clambering back up the rocky top, though an earlier branch left is a shade easier and more direct. Arrival on the neat top is equally exciting, being greeted by an airiness seldom experienced on Lakeland summits. This is a place to soak up the atmosphere while lapping up two outstanding examples of mountain architecture. These are supplied by Gimmer Crag on neighbouring Loft Crag; and Bowfell asserting its full height from Mickleden to summit cairn, truly an exalted profile.

Return to the base of the summit lump and go east on the path skirting the head of the scree run and rising over gentle knolls onto Loft Crag. This is the third of the Langdale Pikes, a less famous cousin of the exalted Stickle brothers, which incidentally are displayed better from here than from any other single vantage point. It also boasts one of Langdale's best known cliffs and a charming summit. The rockface in question is Gimmer Crag, a climbers' favourite that falls away only a short distance below the very summit. This top is another tiny perch, high above a seemingly vertical plunge into Mickleden.

Continue east along the short crest, the path at the end dropping left onto easier ground, but if going to the very end a downward scramble is needed to reach the grassy knoll below. A couple of minutes further and a large cairn in the lowest point marks a path junction. Just in front is the cairned top of Thorn Crag, while the Harrison Stickle path comes in from the left. Here turn sharp right on what immediately becomes a rougher, stony path. This is one of the major Langdales paths, and happily improves in character as the descent unfolds.

Descending the eroded path with care, the way slants left down beneath a ruin and onto a sloping grassy plateau. To the left Harrison Stickle's exquisite summit re-appears. Just short of an abrupt knoll the path swings right to recommence the descent in earnest. It drops to an airy stance above the gullies of Middlefell Buttress, then enjoys a brief terrace along to the left. Running across to a position looking to the great gash of Dungeon Ghyll, just in front, the path then spirals down - one section being particularly rough - to improve as it nears the foot of the ravine: there is a super prospect of the main waterfall. Cross the stream to join another path, and from the stile turn down the wallside path to a kissing-gate. Go left to descend the final enclosure to return to the start.

Pavey Ark from Stickle Tarn

15 LANGDALE PIKES (B)

SUMMITS
HARRISON STICKLE   2415ft/736m
LOFT CRAG   2231ft/680m
PIKE O'STICKLE   2326ft/709m

START Dungeon Ghyll   **Grid ref.** NY 295064

DISTANCE 7 miles/11km   **ASCENT** 2495ft/760m

ORDNANCE SURVEY MAPS
1:50,000 - Landranger 89 **or** 90   1:25,000 - Outdoor Leisure 6

ACCESS Start from the New Hotel, half a mile short of the B5343's end at the Old Hotel. There are National Park and National Trust car parks. Served by bus from Ambleside.

Lakeland's most familiar mountain outline issues an irresistible challenge to all walkers. There are numerous ways to gain their inviting tops, and this route loses nothing of the intimate feel of being amongst the Pikes by seeking the line of least resistance.

S From the drive to the hotel and its hamlet, go straight on through a gate by the side of a cottage. Head up the wallside to a gateway and into an enclosure where the path from the NT car park comes in. Head up between clusters of trees onto the base of the open fell. As the path immediately forks, rise left to a kissing-gate. From it bear right on the rising wallside path, quickly reaching an intervening stile with Dungeon Ghyll itself immediately to the left.

Over the stile is yet another fork. One branch crosses the stream while ours continues straight up with the wall. The surface is largely a rebuilt one, but is a good example of the first-class work done by the National Trust. On a modest brow there is a view ahead to Stickle Gill and its falls, a splendid scene backed by the upper section of the cliff of Pavey Ark. Here the path leaves the wall and rises to the left in a painstakingly restored series of zigzags.

The way is unfailingly simple now as the path winds up to a knoll above the landmark outcrop of Pike How. During this stage Dungeon Ghyll is revealed, with waterfalls and archetypal ravine scenery of the highest order: above, meanwhile, the summit of Harrison Stickle appears as a noble peak, with the rugged Thorn Crag to its left. Views back feature Langdale, Windermere and the northern Coniston Fells.

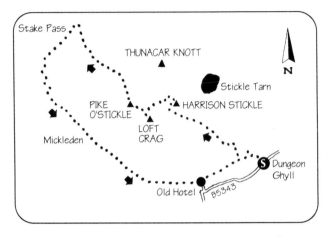

The upper part of the walk takes over, a very gentle stroll on a good and surprisingly not over-used path. Indeed, for a few yards there is the novelty of no path at all. The path is bound directly for the mighty peak of Harrison Stickle, spending quite some time on these uncharacteristically grassy slopes. The path slowly angles left beneath the summit stack to arrive at a narrow defile above the upper falls of the ravine, a super moment. Look back to see the various waters of Windermere, Elterwater, Blea Tarn and Morecambe Bay. Ahead is the pimple of Pike o'Stickle, soon joined by Loft Crag across the ravine.

A brief airy moment soon passes and the path runs on easier ground above the now tame stream, into an upland amphitheatre. Keep on to a fork, where take the right branch for the final stage of the ascent. The path quickly joins a broader one rising from the left to clamber up rocky ground to the surprisingly flat summit area. The highest cairn is just a couple of minutes to the left on this bristly top bedecked with three shapely cairns. To south and east crags guard the top, and it is from here that the most dramatic views are obtained. Three distinctly different features earn a mention, the first being an aerial view of Langdale, its lush, green floor curving away towards Windermere; second is a side-on picture of Pavey Ark hovering above Stickle Tarn; and third an outstanding line-up of lofty peaks hemming in the dalehead.

Most inviting aspect for us is shapely Pike o'Stickle, the walk's other main objective. Retrace steps just a minute or so and then bear right on a path descending easier ground, north-west to a minor saddle between the summit and a small rock tor to the north. At a path junction here turn off left (bound for Pike o'Stickle), descending easy ground to meet the main path again just short of the stream in the amphitheatre.

On crossing, there is an option to detour left for the five-minute pull to the summit of Loft Crag. This is the third of the Langdale Pikes, a less famous cousin of the exalted Stickle brothers, which incidentally are displayed better from here than from any other single vantage point. It also boasts one of Langdale's best known cliffs and a charming summit. The rockface in question is Gimmer Crag, a climbers' favourite that falls away only a short distance below the very summit, which is a tiny perch high above a seemingly vertical plunge into Mickleden.

Resume on the path bound directly for Pike o'Stickle. It runs over knolls to meet the direct path at the head of the great scree shoot where Neolithic man had stone axe 'factories'. The scree run was at one time a Lakeland classic, ensuring a rapid return to the valley for those confident on its sliding stones. Unfortunately they've all slid now, and it is firmly not recommended as a descent route.

Pike o'Stickle's graceful cone thrusts itself skyward from the mass of the mountainside and the barricade of cliffs wrapped around it, and the final climb is as exhilarating as one cares to make it: the normal route climbs to the right before clambering back up the rocky top, though an earlier branch left is a shade easier and more direct. Arrival on the neat top is equally exciting, being greeted by an airiness seldom experienced on Lakeland summits. This is a place to soak up atmosphere, while lapping up two outstanding examples of mountain architecture supplied by Gimmer Crag on neighbouring Loft Crag; and Bowfell asserting its full height from Mickleden to summit cairn, truly an exalted profile.

Return down the main path, there being few options on this rock defended peak. The continuing path now heads north-west bound for the Stake Pass, and after a few stony minutes the Langdales scene is just a memory as the path makes an exceptionally easy descent towards the peaty Martcrag Moor. Straight ahead, the unmistakeable crown of Great Gable slots neatly in beyond intervening ridges. Across Martcrag Moor a final drop leads to the summit of the Stake Pass, a path crossroads marked by a cairn. This is a major crossing of the fells linking Great Langdale and Borrowdale, a regular packhorse route in centuries past.

For Langdale simply turn left and follow the descending path, initially through an upland basin of moraines. A more direct descent follows, on expertly restored zigzags down towards the green floor of Mickleden. The path culminates in a gentle stroll down to meet the Rossett Gill path. Together we run left along the level valley floor between high, rough-walled peaks, ultimately becoming enclosed by walls to run along to the back of the Dungeon Ghyll Old Hotel. While this offers an eminently suitable pause for refreshment, the final stage takes the bridleway straight on along the base of the fell for a good half-mile back to the start.

The Langdale Pikes from Great Langdale (near Chapel Stile)

SUMMITS
SERGEANT MAN   2411ft/735m
HIGH RAISE   2500ft/762m
THUNACAR KNOTT   2372ft/723m

START Dungeon Ghyll   **Grid ref.** NY 295064

DISTANCE 5½ miles/9km   **ASCENT** 2380ft/725m

ORDNANCE SURVEY MAPS
1:50,000 - Landranger 89 **or** 90   1:25,000 - Outdoor Leisure 6

ACCESS Start from the New Hotel, half a mile short of the B5343's end at the Old Hotel. There are National Park and National Trust car parks. Served by bus from Ambleside.

High Raise is true overlord of the Langdale Pikes, but hidden by their bold front it exerts little influence. It is the major fell at the epicentre of Lakeland, and sends convoluted ridges for many miles to north and east. This climb's main objective however is the rocky excrescence of Sergeant Man, a mere pimple on its plateau-edge perhaps, but without which the ascent of High Raise would be a far less worthy experience.

S From the drive to the hotel and its hamlet, go straight on through a gate by the side of a cottage. Head up the wallside to a gateway and into an enclosure behind, where the path from the NT car park comes in. Head up between the small clusters of trees and remain on the restored path by Stickle Gill. The lively beck is soon crossed at a sturdy footbridge. Resume upstream, passing through the centre of an old sheepfold. At the next sidestream, don't cross but take a clear path doubling back up to the right. This too has been repaired, and it provides a splendid ascent on delightful zigzags.

Half way up the path forks, the left branch crossing the stream before climbing to the base of Tarn Crag. Ignore this, and retain the zigzags on a traditional grassy path. The fine peak of Harrison Stickle soars across Stickle Gill, while there is attractive, less dramatic scenery in another gill just to the right of our path. The path remains a gem all the way up to the side of a crumbling enclosure. There are increasing views back over the valley to the Coniston Fells and around to Crinkle Crags at the dalehead.

Passing a ruin on the left, the zigzags fade as the path climbs a grassy tongue. Higher again, the now fading path slants left away from the gill, but can still be followed as it runs above a lesser sidestream onto easier ground. Though very faint now, all is made clear as the walk's principle objective, the rocky dome of Sergeant Man appears. Quite dramatically and suddenly it is followed by the magnificent cliff of Pavey Ark, straight in front, and within seconds Harrison Stickle joins it to form a superlative pairing. Advance in the direction of Sergeant Man to join a clear, level path. At the same time Stickle Tarn appears over to the left.

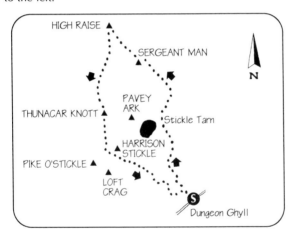

Turn right on this path away from the drama for a short, level tramp. Starting to climb through a stony area, cairns quickly indicate a fork. Bear left, after 25 yards passing a ruined shelter. The path becomes faint here, and soon turns to rise up the inviting grassy slopes between low rock outcrops. One or two cairns aid progress, and the path quickly gains the main ridge which descends from Sergeant Man to divide Langdale from Easedale. If the ascent path is lost, the one running along the broad ridge should easily be found.

First look back at the classic view of Stickle Tarn and its guardian peaks, then ahead to the long skyline of the Fairfield Horseshoe and the Ill Bell ridge. The still thin path meanders pleasantly left, and at one of its cairns Sergeant Man re-appears. The path works round to a better defined dip in the ridge at a small pool: at this point the Helvellyn massif appears to the north. Just a few yards across the ridge, cairns confirm the presence of the main ridge path. Just ahead, the well worn Easedale path also gains the ridge from the other side.

The next ten or so minutes present a choice of paths. The Easedale one is better promoted by cairns guiding onto it, while a thinner one keeps to the Langdale side. Either way, both paths climb the ridge, passing modest outcrops and merging near a sloping slab that offers an interesting 'walk'. Continuing, the summit peak of Sergeant Man beckons more closely, and at the last hollow preceding it, it is revealed just minutes away. It is also revealed for what it really is - a marvellous sham - as near-level ground is seen running away behind it. The path curves around to gain the rocky top, unquestionably a grand place to be. This shapely peak is a notable landmark in distant views, and it lends itself as a useful resting and viewing point in preference to its parent fell. A neatly perched cairn looks down over Bright Beck to the arresting profile of Pavey Ark above Stickle Tarn.

The least interesting part of the view is north-west to High Raise, and this is the direction to take. Of several paths radiating away, the main one crosses rougher ground before a gentle rise to the summit. En route it merges with a line of forlorn fenceposts, and 200 yards short of the top these turn off to the right. The path keeps straight on to gain the OS column and shelter on the rash of stones which give the fell its alternative name of High White Stones.

Being the hub of the district and the highest ground for some distance, High Raise could not fail to command a first-rate panorama. Indeed, it is a challenge to detect the omission of any notable heights. There is interest in all points of the compass, from the nearby Crinkle Crags, Bowfell, Esk Pike and Scafell Pike, round to Great Gable, Pillar, High Stile and Grasmoor. Northwards are the giants of Skiddaw and Blencathra, while the Helvellyn range is unbroken to the east. Of particular note however are more individual features, such as the view up Borrowdale, and the arresting profile of Honister Crag to the north-west.

Leave on the path heading south, bound for the outlines of the Langdale Pikes. For now however they are overtopped by the Coniston Fells, while to the right is majestic Bowfell. A long steady decline leads to a saddle at the head of Bright Beck. Continue straight up the facing slope and onto the gently domed top of Thunacar Knott. A sturdy cairn to the right is passed as the path runs on by the summit cairn. From the cairn its illustrious neighbours the Langdale Pikes are little more than a stone's throw away, yet appear curiously insignificant from 'behind the scenes'. Though this return route charts a course between the Langdale Pikes, a clear day with time to spare will tempt a visit to one or more of these summits for little extra effort. Harrison Stickle, highest and nearest, is the prime candidate, and a thin path runs directly towards it from Thunacar Knott's summit.

From Thunacar Knott the main path continues straight on, declining over easy ground into the basin of Harrison Combe. Here it crosses two paths descending from Harrison Stickle. Simply keep straight on to reach the neck of the combe, alongside the rapidly forming ravines of Dungeon Ghyll. The path also executes an exciting exit, traversing airily above the gill then slanting down contrastingly genteel slopes. This splendid amble beneath Harrison Stickle leads to the rear of the rocky bluff of Pike How. A cleverly rebuilt, steeply winding path then descends right before dropping down by a wall to a stile just above the calmer lower reaches of Dungeon Ghyll. Follow the wall down to a kissing-gate below, then go left down the final enclosure to where the walk began.

The summit of High Raise, looking west

SUMMITS
BOWFELL   2959ft/902m
ROSSETT PIKE   2136ft/651m

START Dungeon Ghyll   **Grid ref.** NY 286061

DISTANCE 9½ miles/15km   **ASCENT** 3020ft/920m

ORDNANCE SURVEY MAPS
1:50,000 - Landranger 89 **or** 90   1:25,000 - Outdoor Leisure 6

ACCESS Start from the Dungeon Ghyll Old Hotel where the B5343 ends at the head of Great Langdale. National Trust car park alongside. Served by bus from Ambleside.

Bowfell is one of the Lakeland 'Giants', a mountain whose summit is gained with greater satisfaction than most, and which projects itself favourably into most views from other parts of the district.

S The main road terminates at a minor crossroads just past the hotel drive. Here a narrow road escapes to cross to Little Langdale, while an unenclosed road begins the walk by heading off through the fields to Stool End. Ahead is a spectacular array of hills, featuring Pike o'Blisco, Crinkle Crags and Bowfell, with the Langdale Pikes quickly revealed to the right. Pass through the farm to a gate onto the open fell, and follow the track rising left with the wall. On a low brow the Band begins its climb to Bowfell, but simply remain with the wallside track.

The level track runs to a sheepfold before joining Oxendale Beck. Ignore the footbridge and remain on the beckside path. Ahead, Crinkle Crags' serrated edge dominates. Keep on past a lively ravine and confluence to rise up a small tongue, finding a footbridge on the beck above another confluence. Cross and climb to the brow above. The main path ascends the bank above the gill, a restored section leading to a good vantage point for the beautiful spout of Whorneyside Force. Looking back, Pike o'Blisco forms a dark, rocky pyramid.

Above the falls the path runs on towards the impending ravine of Hell Gill. Just before it the stream is crossed, quickly followed by crossing the stream from the gorge at its very base. The path then climbs the left side of Hell Gill on a painstakingly restored section before easing out on grass to enjoy cracking views into the upper half of the ravine. Ahead, Bowfell's top appears across this upland basin, a seldom seen angle for such a popular hill: clearly in view is the Band path traversing beneath the rougher upper slopes. Continue up easy ground, closing in on the stream of Buscoe Sike. The path becomes a little faint before re-establishing itself for a final steeper pull to gain the Band path just short of its terminus at Three Tarns.

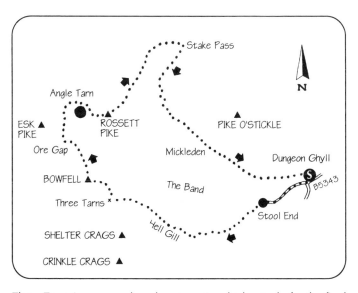

Three Tarns is very much a place to rest and take stock, for the final upper section of Bowfell appears intimidatingly rough. A greater picture for now is the newly revealed prospect across Upper Eskdale to the monumental Scafell massif. On resuming, turn right for the steep stony pull that can be tiresome but is relatively short-lived. The bouldery upper reaches of the mountain are soon be underfoot, with the peak straight ahead, just minutes away. Two cairned paths set forth across the plateau to gain the summit from either east or south, the right-hand one being in more common use.

Bowfell's summit is a crown worthy of such a splendid mountain build-up, a jumble of boulders set at crazy angles, with a cairn leaving nothing to question. Little fault can be found in Bowfell's much vaunted merit as a viewpoint, and certainly there are few better places to while away a lazy half-hour. Valleys and estuaries to the south delightfully balance an outstanding mountain panorama, centrefold of which is the prospect of the mighty Scafell range beyond the south ridge of neighbouring Esk Pike.

A much trodden and amply cairned path sets off just west of north on a direct course for Ore Gap, a gentle stroll that culminates through some bouldery terrain. On a good day this path can be scotched in favour of a lesser one running north to the top of Hanging Knotts before making the short drop to Ore Gap. This affords revealing glimpses of Bowfell's craggy east and north faces as well as a more satisfactory picture of Langdale and the inimitable Pikes.

Ore Gap is unmistakeable by virtue of the dash of red earth on its very crest. From here the summit of Esk Pike is just ten minutes away, and well worth a detour if time and energy permit: a wide path makes the short and undemanding climb to the summit cairn sat just to the north of a large, tor-like outcrop.

From Ore Gap a part cairned path turns down to the right, soon revealing Angle Tarn below. Dropping down to easier ground the path leads around to the main Esk Hause-Rossett Pass thoroughfare. Go right to descend a restored path to stepping-stones over the outflow of the tarn. In its high combe Angle Tarn is a superb example of a mountain pool, and its setting under the brooding northern flanks of Bowfell ensures it sees little winter sun.

At once there is a choice of routes. The direct finish goes straight up the rebuilt path in front to the top of Rossett Pass, thence making a quick but tortuous return to Mickleden by way of Rossett Gill. The next easiest is a short-cut avoiding the crest of Rossett Pike, which branches left immediately after the outflow of the tarn. This runs a clear, near level course around the back of the Pike, merging into the higher path for a steady amble down to the Stake Pass.

The finest option is to include Rossett Pike, so take the path towards the crest of the pass, ahead, then rise left where a thin path makes the shortest of pulls to the summit cairn. The top of the fell supports many rock outcrops, and is the ultimate vantage point for appraising the awesome north-eastern face of Bowfell. A visit to the prominent eastern cairn should be made to gaze down into Mickleden, a precision carved bowl between the Band and the majestic sweep of the Langdale Pikes. From the highest cairn one can witness - audibly, and visibly by peeking over the edge - the excruciating endeavours of pedestrians clambering among the stones of Rossett Gill.

Leave by heading north-east along the ridge-line, with just a faint path to trace. Keeping near to the Mickleden edge earns the more dramatic views, while straight ahead, Langstrath leads the eye beyond Borrowdale to the northern giants of Skiddaw and Blencathra. The way leads over two intervening knolls, though a thin trod skirts the latter (Black Crags) to the left. The path becomes clearer and at numerous stages progress has been helped by the placing of stepping stones across peaty areas. A pool is passed on the left just prior to gaining the summit of the Stake Pass, a path crossroads marked by a cairn.

For Langdale simply turn right and follow the descending path, initially through an upland basin of moraines. A more direct descent follows, on expertly restored zigzags down towards the green floor of Mickleden. The path culminates in a gentle stroll down to meet the Rossett Gill path. Together we run left along the level valley floor between high, rough-walled peaks, ultimately becoming enclosed by walls to run along to the back of the Dungeon Ghyll Old Hotel.

The Langdale Pikes from Flat Crags, Bowfell

PIKE O'BLISCO

SUMMITS
PIKE O'BLISCO   2313ft/705m

START *Dungeon Ghyll*

Grid ref. *NY 285061*

DISTANCE *5 miles/8km*

ASCENT *2200ft/670m*

ORDNANCE SURVEY MAPS
*1:50,000 - Landranger 89 **or** 90   1:25,000 - Outdoor Leisure 6*

ACCESS *Start from the Dungeon Ghyll Old Hotel where the B5343 ends at the head of Great Langdale. National Trust car park alongside. Served by bus from Ambleside.*

An important player on the Langdale stage, Pike o'Blisco is a shapely mountain in the midst of loftier, equally shapely mountains. When the crowds set forth to conquer Bowfell or the Langdale Pikes, the discerning walker will turn his eyes here: he may not be alone, but neither will he get trampled underfoot.

S The main road terminates at a minor crossroads just past the hotel drive. Here a narrow road escapes to cross to Little Langdale, while an unenclosed road begins the walk by heading off through the fields to Stool End. Ahead is a spectacular array of hills, featuring Pike o'Blisco, Crinkle Crags and Bowfell, with the Langdale Pikes quickly revealed to the right. Pass through the farm to a gate onto the open fell, and follow the track rising left with the wall. On a low brow the Band begins its climb to Bowfell, but simply remain with the wallside track.

The track runs a level course to a sheepfold, before joining Oxendale Beck. Just upstream its stony course is crossed by a footbridge, and after a couple of minutes on the grassy bank, a cairn signals the start of the well trodden climb up Pike o'Blisco's flank. Ahead, the ravines under Crinkle Crags provide much interest, and the path itself skirts a rough section of Browney Gill. Much of the path has been restored, and rising past the cliffs of Black Wars the gradient steadily lets up.

The broad saddle occupied by Red Tarn between Pike o'Blisco and Crinkle Crags is approached as the path levels out. When it forks, the main branch goes right to the outflow of Red Tarn. Keeping straight on (left), the path fades as it runs to a major path junction. The left arm resumes the climbing, a zealously cairned path covering the last enjoyable 650 feet up the uniform slope to the summit.

The summit is a colourful place in keeping with the nature of the fell. Cairns of equally impressive dimensions occupy the two highest points, with that to the north stealing the glory on both altitude and merit, particularly as a viewpoint. A splendid contrast in the view is formed by the numerous sheets of water in the lowlands south-east, and the magnificently sculptured precipices and tops of Crinkle Crags and Bowfell ranged beyond the deep chasm of the headwaters of Oxendale. Especially appealing is the map-like Dungeon Ghyll picture of hotels, farms and green fields.

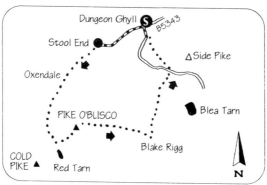

On eventually departing, the path to take is that heading east from the peaty depression between the two tops. The path quickly starts a rapid descent, involving minor scrambles down three seperate rock bands to gain the gentler terrain of the broad east ridge. The path remains on the Great Langdale side of the ridge to arrive above the steep and rough beginning of the main and fastest descent, in the company of Redacre Gill. Far below is Dungeon Ghyll with the Langdale Pikes rising as impressively as ever behind.

In good weather only, the usual descent with its initially trying section can be avoided by bearing off on a faint path to the right. Along the ridge the easternmost top of Blake Rigg beckons, so quickly leave the

67

trod (which is also aiming to descend), and rise to find a slender, cairned way passing by a sizeable pool. Go left on this faint trod for a lovely stride on the broad, grassy ridge, passing south of the cairn on Bleaberry Knott to gain the better defined Blake Rigg just beyond. Another fine cairn marks its highest point, only a short way to the east of which a wall of cliffs brings proceedings to a spectacularly abrupt conclusion. Eastwards Little Langdale Tarn is well seen nestling in its valley, leading the eye to a more distant Windermere.

Bowfell from Pike o'Blisco

The way off strikes north along the knobbly ridge aiming for the top of the Blea Tarn road. Keeping the receding cliffs safely down to the right, a splendid descent can be enjoyed on pathless grass between craggy outcrops. The views of the Pikes continue to improve, earning better perspective as height is lost. There are also some charming views of Blea Tarn backed by Lingmoor Fell. Windswept trees stand over the crumbling wall on the right, before a final, intervening knoll is rounded to find the road summit just below. Anyone feeling energetic might now choose to join up with the Lingmoor Fell route, adding a further 7 miles (see WALK 20).

Directly across the road is a stile, from where a path turns sharp left in front of a memorial seat. The path descends in the company of a wall before passing through a small plantation and then a slender wooded bank to enter the National Trust campsite. Turn left along its drive and out onto the road, then right to finish.

```
                    SUMMITS
   CRINKLES SOUTH TOP   2736ft/834m
        CRINKLE CRAGS   2818ft/859m
        SHELTER CRAGS   2674ft/815m
```

START Dungeon Ghyll

Grid ref. NY 286061

DISTANCE 7½ miles/12km

ASCENT 2790ft/850m

ORDNANCE SURVEY MAPS
1:50,000 - Landranger 89 **or** 90
1:25,000 - Outdoor Leisure 6

ACCESS Start from the Dungeon Ghyll Old Hotel where the B5343 ends at the head of Great Langdale. National Trust car park alongside. Served by bus from Ambleside.

Crinkle Crags is one of Lakeland's finest mountains, being regularly traversed and overlooking a famous dalehead, yet must play second fiddle to its partner Bowfell. Crinkle Crags is probably climbed more in conjunction with Bowfell than in its own right, yet it boasts a handful of summits on its mile-long ridge, and the full crossing, omitting nothing, is one of the district's most rewarding walks.

S The main road terminates at a minor crossroads just past the hotel drive. Here a narrow road escapes to cross to Little Langdale, while an unenclosed road begins the walk by heading off through the fields to Stool End. Ahead is a spectacular array of hills, featuring Pike o'Blisco, Crinkle Crags and Bowfell, with the Langdale Pikes quickly revealed to the right. Pass through the farm to a gate onto the open fell, and follow the track rising left with the wall. On a low brow the Band begins its climb to Bowfell, but simply remain with the wallside track.

The track runs a level course to a sheepfold before joining Oxendale Beck. Just upstream its stony course is crossed by a footbridge, and after a couple of minutes on the grassy bank, a cairn signals the start of the well trodden climb up Pike o'Blisco's flank. Ahead, the ravines under Crinkle Crags provide much interest, and the path itself skirts a rough section of Browney Gill. Much of the path has been restored, and rising past the cliffs of Black Wars the gradient steadily lets up. At a fork bear right to run along to the outflow from Red Tarn. Here begins a long, easy pull on a wide path, and above the minor outlier of Great Knott the way becomes gentler still. The character of the walk changes suddenly as the southern end of the true Crinkles ridge is gained: prepare for a mile to remember. To the west the Scafell group is magnificently ranged across Upper Eskdale, with the familiar Langdale scene still to the right.

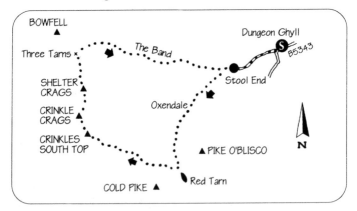

The Crinkles South Top is quickly underfoot, and its cairn is a splendid place to take stock. Immediately ahead rises the highest and greatest Crinkle, Long Top. Before it can be gained, however, the celebrated obstacle known as the Bad Step reveals itself on descent to the windswept col. Walkers overfaced by the prospect should note that their predecessors have created a well-stamped escape path. This runs left, descending a few feet before a stony climb culminates as a grassy one onto Long Top, just west of the summit cairn.

The Bad Step is really only potentially 'bad' in descent, for it gives the simplest of scrambles from its foot. The good holds of the solid rock to the right of the chockstone-filled gully lead to easier ground above. Within seconds it's all over, and within minutes the summit of Crinkle Crags is gained. For a break from the ridge, saunter westwards along the broad spur of Long Top, which provides good depth to views across upper Eskdale. Combining the stunning views with the quality of one's own location, the magic of the mountains is truly experienced. Additionally, a refreshing balance is given to Crinkle Crags' views by the rich valley scenery, with Langdale, Eskdale and the Duddon all appearing as broad green straths.

Resume this classic crossing on the path north, egged on by the statuesque Bowfell. Almost immediately the path drops to a broad grassy sward atop the spectacular gash of Mickle Door, a great scree gully. The third, more rounded Crinkle hovers over it, while the other two stand just beyond, all on the Langdale side of the ridge. Though the path weaves round them, they scarcely deserve exclusion: all are within a stone's throw and should be visited in clear weather. Beyond them the path makes a more discernible climb to the slightly lower but greater upthrust of Shelter Crags, whose top is only yards up to the left and emphatically merits a visit. Immediately below, a delightful little tarn makes a splendid foreground to Bowfell. Still a succession of delights, the path runs largely downhill to the depression of Three Tarns, a major staging post.

After an appraisal of Bowfell's steep face, take the cairned path down to the right to commence the long, easy angled descent offered by the Band. This immensely popular path first traverses across the upper flanks of Bowfell to gain this ridge emanating from its summit plateau. A near-level section precedes the descent proper, during which the Langdale scene is presented in exquisite fashion. Keep to the path towards the bottom as it swings down to avoid an unseen crag, ultimately meeting the outward route by the intake wall. Turn left to retrace steps back through Stool End and out through the fields to the start.

Bowfell from Long Top, Crinkle Crags

> **SUMMITS**
> *LINGMOOR FELL   1538ft/469m*

START *Dungeon Ghyll*

Grid ref. *NY 286061*

DISTANCE *8 miles/13km*

ASCENT *1600ft/487m*

ORDNANCE SURVEY MAPS
1:50,000 - Landranger 90   1:25,000 - Outdoor Leisure 6 & 7

ACCESS *Start from the Dungeon Ghyll Old Hotel at the head of Great Langdale. National Trust car park alongside. Served by bus from Ambleside. A useful option is to catch the bus to Dungeon Ghyll and just do the fellwalking section of the route, finishing at Elterwater to meet the bus again.*

Of Lingmoor Fell's twin attributes of character and location, the latter is pre-eminent as it twists and turns to forever divide majestic Great Langdale and homely Little Langdale.

S   From the car park return to the main road, then turn right and sharp left. At the first bend a stile and footpath sign point the way into the National Trust campsite on the left. At the first opportunity turn off the drive into the trees on the right, where a footpath rises to leave the site via a wooded bank. Continue straight up through a second patch of woodland onto the open fell. A steep climb then ensues in the company of a wall, with stunning retrospective views of the Langdale Pikes. The slope eases out to arrive at the summit of the Blea Tarn road connecting Great Langdale and Little Langdale.

Without joining the road pass behind a memorial seat to a gap in the wall ahead, from where a path contours through bracken parallel with the road below. Up to the left are the craggy flanks of Lingmoor's underling, Side Pike. In this bowl in the hills sits Blea Tarn, and the lonely white-walled cottage by the road is Bleatarn House, Wordsworth's 'one bare dwelling; one abode, no more!'. Beyond the tarn are the northern Coniston Fells of Wetherlam and Swirl How. At a stile a path from the road is met to climb steeply to the saddle at the base of Side Pike's rocky boss.

Turning away from the forbidding crag, a pleasant green path heads up to the right alongside the sturdy wall. The Langdale Pikes are seen at their brilliant best to the left. After a short climb the wall is crossed at a stile, and the main path continues up the other side, taking a series of stony outcrops in its stride. The going eases amid heather and rocky ground, and a branch rises left to a cairned knoll: this is the last spectacular viewpoint for the Langdale Pikes. Across near-level ground the summit now awaits, beyond a beckoning false top. In the company of a fence the re-united paths tramp a gentle high-level course, with Lingmoor Tarn appearing in its colourful hollow down to the left. The cairned false top is passed before arrival at the large cairn that well confirms the summit's superiority.

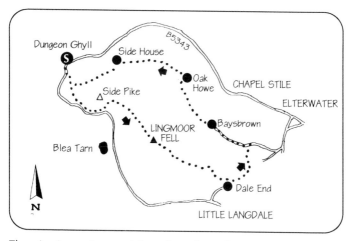

The view's great appeal is variety, from the extensive waters of Windermere to the magnificent array of mountains enclosing Great Langdale. To the north meanwhile, at our very feet, the green fields of the dale are sheltered by the curving arm of Blea Rigg extending from the Pikes down to Silver How. There is a glimpse of Coniston Water through the Tilberthwaite gap, while Little Langdale is well seen beneath the fells of the Greenburn Horseshoe.

Leave the top by crossing the adjacent stile and heading away with the fence. The quickly returning wall appears in style as it rolls assertively on in the fashion of Hadrian's Wall. Little height is lost as the ridge of the fell continues south-eastwards, a thin path remaining with or close to the wall. After a rise to a slate cairn on the right, the bracken level is reached and the path immediately becomes very distinct. Various evidences of defunct slate quarrying activity are passed, though the most impressive, an alarming, gaping cliff face on the very ridge top, will be missed unless a brief detour is made to peer - with extreme caution - down it. On the floor of Great Langdale, Chapel Stile resembles an Alpine, chocolate box village.

The Langdale Pikes from Lingmoor Fell

Passing a ruinous stone hut and more spoil, the inviting green pathway weaves down through the bracken: ahead is the small lake of Elterwater, seldom seen to advantage from the fellpaths. At a wide green crossroads keep straight on, just after which is an opportunity to detour out to a prominent cairn above Bield Crag, a classic Little Langdale viewpoint. The path continues down, swinging sharply right before a wall corner, then steepening to zigzag stylishly down in the fashion of these old quarry tracks. The hamlet of Little Langdale is outspread below, while Little Langdale Tarn makes a cameo appearance further to the right. The path drops to a stile in the bottom corner, then swinging left the path meets a further stile before joining the unsurfaced Elterwater-Little Langdale road above Dale End Farm.

Turn left along the rough road until it descends into a wood, then branch left on a bridleway (for Elterwater, continue straight down onto the road at the edge of the village). The bridleway rises slightly to a miniature pass in the trees before heading tidily off between crumbling walls. The path then descends to cross a woodland track to arrive at an isolated dwelling. A surfaced road is joined, and this is followed to the left for a long woodland walk to Baysbrown Farm. The final approach is a splendid scene, emerging from the wood to see the farm backed by the cliff of Pavey Ark.

A roughly surfaced road takes up the journey beyond the farm to rise into more woodland. As it turns to climb steeply, forsake this old quarry road in favour of a bridleway heading on through the trees. The way runs on and then down to approach the next set of buildings, at Oak Howe. At the first barn, turn sharp left to continue up-dale on a delightful walled path. The full complement of Langdale Pikes now reappear in quick succession.

At the demise of the enclosed way, the path forges on along the base of Lingmoor Fell. Look out for the pinnacle of Oak Howe Needle projecting from the fellside high above. The way runs on, keeping above the intake wall and with Great Langdale Beck in its deep channelled course below. Dungeon Ghyll appears with the Langdale Pikes rising protectively behind, a classic scene. Past a sheepfold in a wall corner the rebuilt path strikes down a large pasture then alongside the wall to Side House.

The right of way turns into the yard and out to the road at the New Hotel, but a permissive path will take us back to the campsite. Without crossing the little stream rise up the field to a ladder-stile in the wall ahead. The final section crosses several fields on a generally clear course along the base of Side Pike. On petering out above a narrow plantation, slant down to the marshy far corner where a stile is found. Just below it is a kissing-gate into the campsite. Turn left along the access road to retrace the walk's opening steps.

SUMMITS	
WETHERLAM	*2503ft/763m*
BLACK SAILS	*2444ft/745m*
SWIRL HOW	*2631ft/802m*
GREAT CARRS	*2575ft/785m*

START Little Langdale   **Grid ref.** NY 316033

DISTANCE 8½ miles/13½km   **ASCENT** 3085ft/940m

ORDNANCE SURVEY MAPS
1:50,000 - Landranger 90   1:25,000 - Outdoor Leisure 6

ACCESS Start from the centre of the hamlet, by the Three Shires Inn. Parking is very limited: there is a little space by the phone box, otherwise there is much better parking on a wider section of road at the eastern end of the hamlet by a terraced row.

The Greenburn Horseshoe makes an outstanding excursion, from the pastures of a peaceful valley to a magnificent skyline walk.

S Leave the road by the junction to Tilberthwaite (unfit for cars) just west of the pub. Descending this surfaced lane look for a kissing-gate on the right part way down. From it a path climbs some steps and crosses the field to another kissing-gate. Ahead the Greenburn Horseshoe awaits, with Wetherlam dominant and Great Carrs set back to its right: Swirl How, the kingpin, remains elusive until gaining Wetherlam's summit. Keep straight on, and the way winds down with Slater's Bridge in view below. The path descends to an absolute gem of a setting, where this charismatic arched footbridge is found in tandem with a clapper-bridge.

The path then crosses the field beyond to join a rough lane beneath quarry spoil heaps. Turn right to the cottage at Low Hall Garth and the way climbs up behind, on past High Hall Garth to emerge onto the open fell. Down to the right is Little Langdale Tarn: as soon as the track heads off, Pike o'Stickle appears with style over to the right. The track heads away to join the firmer track of an unclassified road linking Fell Foot to Tilberthwaite. Advance just 100 yards along this and take a broad fork left. This old miners' track runs a splendid course, with excellent views of our return ridge, Wet Side Edge, and across to Pike o'Blisco and the Langdale Pikes.

The track runs unfailingly on to reach a gate in a wall. With Greenburn Beck for company advance on a few minutes further to arrive at the site of Greenburn Copper Works. Due to a more recent demise than most of the district's mining operations, there remain some sizeable ruins here, inside which is the pit once occupied by a waterwheel. Please remember it is not advisable to stray far off the paths in this area as hidden dangers lurk, not least of which are some vertical mineshafts.

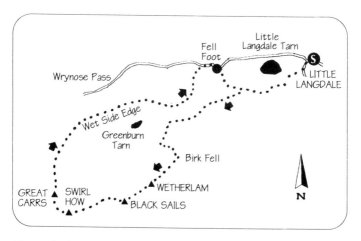

Alongside the ruins turn left up the very distinct course of an incline, where a tramway once operated. A fainter grassy way follows this course up to a small area of spoil, passing a deep, water-filled shaft on the right. Although the grassy incline continues directly up the steepening slopes to a spoil heap high above (with the dip of Birkfell Hause above that), instead slant right, aided by an occasional cairn, to find a green track forming. It can be seen much clearer slanting up the fell just ahead, and is easily picked out and followed. Part way up it turns sharply left and makes a delightful slant on a well engineered way to reach that spoil heap without effort.

Looking back, Greenburn Tarn is revealed as a shadow of its former self since its dam was breached, while northwards are views over Blea Tarn to the Helvellyn, Fairfield, Red Screes and Ill Bell groups; additionally, Crinkle Crags and Bowfell are seen across the Wrynose Pass. Back on the path, to the right is the cause of the spoil: a dark, dripping mine level. Continue a few steps further to a long line of spoil and scree: it is baffling to observe that someone has seen fit to build a series of close-knit cairns immediately below us, to send a steep and stony path straight down, in ignorance of our time-honoured way!

Now however take advantage of the cairns as they send a stony path climbing away, then doubling back to a second level site just above. Again helped by cairns, rise to a third and final level, from where the path slants gently left, rising increasingly faintly to arrive on Birkfell Hause. It matters little if the upper section of path is lost, as the ridge cannot be missed. This is a cracking moment as new views open out to the south, looking over Tilberthwaite Gill to charming country leading to Morecambe Bay.

Now the nature of the climb completely changes. Simply turn right on the well worn path, which scales unfailingly and exuberantly the ridge of Wetherlam Edge. Those with an eye for rock will find a number of inviting and very easy scrambling opportunities on a line to the left of the path. The going eases only as the cairn appears just ahead, occupying a rocky knoll upon a small plateau. Only at this point does the continuing walk reveal itself, with the walk's other major peak, Swirl How, finally revealed ahead, along with the other Coniston Fells. For a note on the view, please see page 83.

Heading west a clear path quickly forms, descending gently to a saddle before the intervening Black Sails. The path completely ignores this lesser fell by clinging to the Greenburn edge of the broad ridge, but in clear weather it is worth a few minutes of anyone's time to detour onto the summit. A good cairn occupies a better defined top. This brings a super bird's-eye view down onto Levers Water backed by the main Coniston ridge, with Coniston Water itself now seen almost in its entirety.

Slant north-west to regain the path, which drops quickly onto Swirl Hause. This is a fine, atmospheric example of a mountain pass. Continue straight up the other side, enjoying a climb up the ridge of Prison Band, which despite looking aggressive from Black Sails, is no more than a steep walk with a hand kept on stand-by for occasional steadying. It leads unfailingly to Swirl How's obelisk of a summit cairn, reaching all of seven feet into the sky and misleadingly appearing to teeter on the brink of an unbroken plunge to the Greenburn valley.

This zenith of the walk is a particularly grand place to be. Despite being marginally overtopped by the Old Man, Swirl How is undeniably the kingpin of the Coniston Fells, with ridges radiating to all points of the compass. On arrival, new features revealed westwards include the delicate peak of Dow Crag, just across our group, and a section of the Duddon Valley.

Resume on the stony path curving around the rim of Broad Slack, rising to find Great Carrs' summit underfoot within ten minutes. On the re-ascent a memorial cairn might be spotted just 30 yards down the gentle slope to the left. Incorporating twisted metal it recalls a tragic wartime crash when all eight crew of a Halifax bomber were killed during a night navigation exercise.

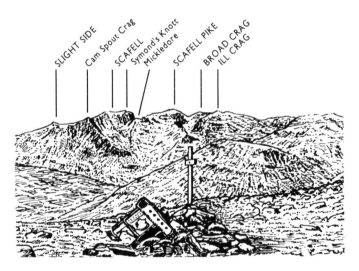

Looking north-west to the Scafell massif from the aircraft wreck on Great Carrs

Arrival on the day's finest summit is a moment to savour, for the cairn is found to balance on an upthrust of rock immediately above an unshackled plunge into Greenburn. Across the gap of Broad Slack the uncompromising face of Swirl How adds further to the drama of the scene. The outstanding panorama to the north features all six of England's 3000-footers amongst an all-star cast.

Leave the summit on a cairned path continuing the previous line, descending easy terrain along the forming ridge of Wet Side Edge. There are good views back to find the pyramid of Harter Fell now appeared from behind Grey Friar: the floor of Wrynose Bottom is also well seen. The path leaves the edge for a section in which it absorbs the Grey Friar path, though a fainter green way clings more faithfully to the Greenburn side. The main path also returns to the edge before a junction sends a more popular branch left down to the summit of the Wrynose Pass.

Continue on the edge, now in solitude on an inviting grassy trod. Remember to keep casting an eye back to the imposing twosome of Swirl How and Great Carrs. The path descends uneventfully, very easily and with outstanding views to reach the bouldery Rough Crags. Steep crags break up the flanks to the north, so keep to the path which drops down to the right. A sloping, grassy plateau completes the descent. There are two options here: the first is simply to take a green path down through the bracken to the right, crossing Greenburn Beck to return on the outward path.

Alternatively, stay on the broad ridge and drop left, passing between an island enclosure and the intake wall as several strategically placed cairns hint at a vague path. Descend to cross the youthful river Brathay just short of the intake. A neatly constructed cairn on a boulder on the knoll opposite sends a faint way the few yards further to a gate/stile in the wall corner beyond. A path runs right with the wallside to a gate/stile onto the foot of the Wrynose Pass, immediately beneath Castle Howe.

Turn right down the road, passing the characterful farm of Fell Foot. Just beyond, leave the road at a stone arched bridge on the right and follow the rough road to the cottage at Bridge End. Remain on this old road as it slants up to absorb our outward route. Going left, remember to fork left again after 100 yards to return to the start.

```
                    SUMMITS
        WETHERLAM    2503ft/763m
```

START Tilberthwaite   **Grid ref.** NY 306009

DISTANCE 5½ miles/9km   **ASCENT** 2065ft/630m

ORDNANCE SURVEY MAPS
1:50,000 - Landranger 90 & 96   1:25,000 - Outdoor Leisure 6

ACCESS Start from a large parking area by old quarries at Low Tilberthwaite, on a cul-de-sac road a short mile north of the A593 Coniston-Ambleside road. The main road carries a bus service.

This member of the close-knit Coniston family is something of a loner, and the one which is most regularly the sole objective of an outing. Wetherlam is riddled with evidence of mineral workings, and while abandoned slate quarries are evident at either end of the walk, the sites of former copper mines add much interest to this fine climb. Indeed, as much of the walk is related to these aspects as to the ascent proper. Remember, of course, that it is dangerous to investigate too closely.

This first paragraph details an alternative start which delves into the heart of the Tilberthwaite Gill ravine, a National Park Access Area, before joining the main route. Steps up the rear of the car park lead to a slate track between spoil, climbing past a big quarry hole on the left and the start of a ravine on the right. At a fork by a ruined slate hut, a level green track branches right, running to a footbridge in the gill. There is a chance to look deeper into the heart of the ravine here. Across the bridge a path climbs steeply to join a broad miners' track.

S From the car park go north along the road over Yewdale Beck, and turn off at the cottages at Low Tilberthwaite. Note the splendid example of a spinning gallery. Take the track along the front of the cottages, then climbing steeply uphill. Quickly take the path signed left, which curves round to cross a beck before commencing a long slant up the fellside. A dark, dripping mine level is quickly passed and the views open out. Little Holme Fell stands just across the spoil heaps, while back to the north are the Fairfield, Red Screes and Ill Bell ridges.

This old miners' track climbs above the ravine of Tilberthwaite Gill (being joined by the alternative start) to emerge past its wooded environs and more fully reveal our mountain waiting in front, a great craggy wall. The skyline climbing to it on the right is to be the ascent route. At a cairn the path forks: in front it runs on to numerous levels and shafts of the former copper mines, but the route forks right to slant gently up the fell. Passing some ruins amid further evidence of old workings, it curves above the hollow of Dry Cove Bottom, then up above the higher and moister Dry Cove Moss.

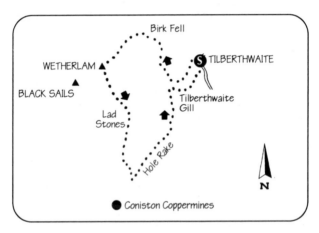

Ignoring a cairned branch right at a ruined stone shed, advance another 100 yards to just short of a ruined building at another mining site. The footpath branches right to climb a well restored route to a knoll by some trees and a wall. Cairns send the path up past scree spoil and the final level and deep shaft, then it winds agreeably up onto the ridge of Birk Fell. The wispish path winds along to the left to gain the true ridge top, being greeted by super views north to the likes of Pike o'Blisco, Glaramara, the Langdale Pikes and Helvellyn. Just a few minutes further and the dip of Birkfell Hause is reached, with Greenburn Tarn down to the right.

Now the nature of the climb completely changes. Simply forge on up the well worn path, which scales unfailingly and exuberantly the rough and rocky ridge of Wetherlam Edge. Those with an eye for rock will find a number of inviting and very easy scrambling opportunities on a line to the left of the path. The going eases only as the cairn appears just ahead, occupying a rocky knoll on a small plateau.

Wetherlam's detachment from the Coniston group permits richly varied views. To the north the great mountain barriers of the Scafells, Bowfell and Helvellyn are ranged majestically, with the adjacent Coniston Fells forming a solid wall with their impressive eastern faces. At one's feet, however, is what makes Wetherlam special, the wonderfully contrasting low country stretching from Tilberthwaite over to Windermere. Intermittently lavishly wooded and bracken covered foothills, dappled with plentiful sheets of water culminating in England's largest lake, ensure an altogether memorable landscape.

Leave the top by heading south past a large cairn, with a path quickly forming. This runs above a couple of airy drops towards Dry Cove Moss, then ambles less eventfully down the broad ridge of Lad Stones, with Coniston Water ahead. The path is largely clear though becomes curiously faint on a steeper section. The walking is exceptionally easy as the path runs down, savouring a super array of Coniston's rugged fells on the right, with Levers Water appearing beneath them. Suddenly and unexpectedly the path swings left off the ridge to avoid steep ground ahead. By now the return path is clearly evident below, running a level course along the edge of Yewdale Moss. The descent path again becomes occasionally faint, but drops pleasantly to join the old quarrymans' path above a steep drop to the Coppermines Valley.

For Coniston turn right down it, but otherwise go left through the pass of Hole Rake, rising briefly to run on past a reedy pool. Evidence of quarrying is passed as this splendid green way drops gently into the amphitheatre of Yewdale Moss, revealing more of the ascent route as it goes. Faced by a small marsh the original track crosses it faintly then runs clearly on the base of the fell past several old mine levels, but the more commonly used path swings round to the right and contours round to approach the head of Tilberthwaite Gill. The paths rejoin at the crossing of Crook Beck, the southerly feeder. Here swinging right, the way runs downstream on a clear traverse well above the ravine, and passing a mine level. The path then descends to the gaping quarry hole and down between the spoil to steps back down to the car park.

HOLME FELL

SUMMITS
HOLME FELL   1040ft/317m

START *Hodge Close*   **Grid ref.** *NY 315015*

DISTANCE *4 miles/6½km*   **ASCENT** *600ft/183m*

ORDNANCE SURVEY MAPS
1:50,000 - Landranger 90, Landranger 96
1:25,000 - Outdoor Leisure 7

ACCESS *Start on old slate quarry land on the roadside between Holme Ground and Hodge Close, 1½ miles off the A593 Coniston-Ambleside road. Ample parking. Buses run along the main road, which the walk comes within two minutes of part way through.*

In the shadow of Wetherlam, Holme Fell does its best, despite its physical limitations, to match up to the standards of its more illustrious elders. In its limited confines nothing is wasted, for crags, woods, knobbly outcrops, zones of heather, green paths through tall bracken, several reservoirs rehabilitated by nature's healing hand, and quarries both defunct and working are all crammed into this little wedge of land.

S A quite remarkable and dangerous feature at the very start are the monstrous holes of Parrock and Hodge Close Quarries. With their clean slate walls and deep pools these abandoned chasms are the playground of rock climbers and divers, and humble walkers can venture down through Parrock Quarry, from the far end, to an arch linking into the other quarry. On a more traditional note, the Langdale Pikes are also well seen from the start point.

The walk begins from a small ruin at the southern end of Hodge Close Quarry, the first one reached on the drive in. Take the stony path running to a gate into the wooded lower slopes of Holme Fell. Turn right on the wallside track, quickly arriving at another gate beneath some small spoil heaps. Just past them, leave the track on a lesser one slanting back up to the left. At the old quarry site a sizeable quarry hole appears ahead, and several paths diverge.

Of the two paths to the right, take the left-hand one rising steeply then running on past a small marsh to arrive on the shore of a tarn. This extensive sheet of water is a reservoir that served the quarries, but now does an admirable job serving nature. Already the summit is plainly in view, ahead and to the right of the prominent peak of Ivy Crag. A path crosses the outflow and runs along the right bank. At the end it bears off to the left to rise, less clearly in part, to the prominent nick of Uskdale Gap on the skyline. This impressively named saddle is marked by a cairn and the vestiges of an old wall.

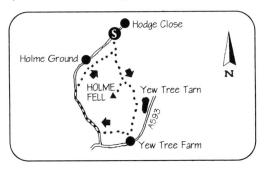

Up to the right, a path climbs towards the summit. An obvious detour should be made to the large cairn on Ivy Crag, from where the summit of the fell beckons across a minor col. The elongated ridge is gained by a weakness in the craggy rim defending it, and the highest cairn stands to the southern end on a tilted slab. The fine panorama extends from the great bulk of Wetherlam immediately adjacent, to the beautifully wooded low country around Tarn Hows. Of particular note is the full length view of Coniston Water stretching finger-like into the distance. To the north is a superb array of mountains, from those around the head of Langdale to the long, gentler skylines of the Helvellyn, Fairfield and Ill Bell ridges.

Return to Uskdale Gap and turn down the path to the right. Soon entering a wood, it makes a pleasurable, sustained drop, generally angling to the right. During this a large fellside clearing affords a good prospect over Yew Tree Tarn just below. At the bottom of the slope a level path is met at a cairn and massive boulder. Turning right along it, the next mile or so is on a concession path marked by white arrows. It quickly leaves the trees at a gate, from where it goes left a few yards before resuming a level course through mixed terrain. A farm track forms to soon arrive at a gate just above Yew Tree Farm and the main road.

Don't pass through the gate but turn right above the fence, and the ensuing wall keeps us on a path along the base of the fell. Ahead, the craggy Yewdale Fells are backed by lofty Wetherlam. After an intervening gate a good track materialises to undulate along beneath the craggy southern buttresses that belie Holme Fell's modest stature. Still intermittently waymarked, the way becomes a wonderful green track through lovely surroundings to emerge onto the Hodge Close road at Shepherd's Bridge.

Turn right along the road for a long half-mile in the company of lively Yewdale Beck. After a rise away from it, a bridleway sign is reached on the right. From it a good track rises steadily with a wall through woodland, then across an open pasture with the farm at Holme Ground on the road below. A green track climbs from the farm to a hairpin bend: take the upper branch rising to a wall. This leads to a gate back into the trees. Ahead is a brief cameo of Helvellyn and Fairfield. This now firmer track leads on to quickly rejoin the outward route just short of the start.

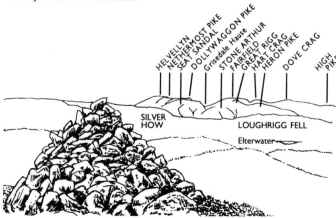

Looking north-east from Ivy Crag

> **SUMMITS**
> *BROWN PIKE* 2237ft/682m
> *DOW CRAG* 2552ft/778m

START Coniston   **Grid ref.** NY 289970

DISTANCE 6 miles/9½km   **ASCENT** 1885ft/575m

ORDNANCE SURVEY MAPS
1:50,000 - Landranger 96 **or** Landranger 97
1:25,000 - Outdoor Leisure 6

ACCESS Start from the surfaced end of the Walna Scar Road, a steep mile out of the village. It is found south of the bridge by the Black Bull, where a back road climbs past the Sun Hotel before embracing the steep gradients of a narrowing road that eventually expires at the forever opening and shutting 'Fell Gate'. Coniston is served by bus from Ambleside.

With a monumental rock face, a naked rock summit, a gloomy tarn and several lesser tops, Dow Crag boasts many of the features that make a good mountain. There is no doubting its principal attraction though, for the outstanding wall of dark cliffs and gullies brooding over the equally sombre Goat's Water is one of Lakeland's finest sights. The two usual walkers' routes to the summit reveal stunning views of it, and combined into this circular tour leave the visitor comprehensively illuminated.

S Of the two unsurfaced tracks heading away, take that to the left. This is the continuation of the Walna Scar Road, an historic trade route linking Coniston with the Duddon Valley. It provides an exceptionally undemanding climb to the 2000ft contour. The way is foolproof, and the reedy pool of Boo Tarn is first of numerous features of interest along the way, just past the access road climbing to Bursting Stone Quarry.

Making early efforts to gain height (perhaps encouraged by the appearance of Brown Pike, which is to be the first summit of the walk, high in front) the track climbs through rock gateways, and after crossing a sidestream a large cairn marks what will be our return path descending from unseen Goat's Water. Just past here Dow Crag comes into view, and the peak is henceforth rarely out of sight: as the walk unfolds it can be appreciated from many angles. A little further and the track crosses Torver Beck at Cove Bridge. With the beck tumbling below, this former packhorse bridge makes a good foreground to Dow Crag's mighty cliffs.

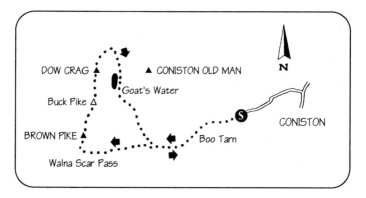

Immediately above us is Brown Pike, and the path quickly rises to the base of its slopes. A branch right is a former quarrymans' path to Blind Tarn Quarry, and also offers a diversion to the delightfully located Blind Tarn. On the left of our track, meanwhile, a parallel section of old green road is evident. Continuing, an intriguing free-standing shelter stands by the track just minutes before it gains the crest of the Walna Scar Pass. A sudden vista of wilder country presents itself to the west, featuring the rocky pyramid of Harter Fell, and to its right, the majestic massif of the Scafells.

As the old packhorse route is sent on its way down to the Duddon Valley, steps turn to the flank on the right. A broad path climbs steeply to the cairn and shelter on the minor top of Brown Pike. Sweeping views beyond the Duddon Valley contrast nicely with the appearance of the remarkably circular Blind Tarn in a delectable hollow several hundred feet below: note the absence of an outflowing stream.

Ahead waits the next top of Buck Pike, and it is a steady haul onto its insignificant top. This heralds the dramatic appearance of Dow Crag's summit peak, and brings Great Carrs and Swirl How into view across Goat's Hause. Remember to look back for a fine picture of Blind Tarn nestling beneath Buck Pike. From this point a simple stroll leads along the ridge to beckoning Dow Crag, the final section increasingly illuminated by striking views down into the dark gullies high above Goat's Water: quite outstanding rock architecture. Neighbouring Coniston Old Man looms large across the hollow of the tarn.

The summit oozes atmosphere, an upthrust of naked rock pointing boldly skywards and demanding a minor clamber to claim it. There is neither need nor room for a cairn. This is no place to leave in a hurry, for it demands respect and time to savour its structure and setting. A survey of the surrounding country is likely to instil the scene in the southern sector into one's memory rather than the mountains, for while the Scafell group is well presented, the arrangement of the softer landscapes offers more, with Morecambe Bay, Coniston Water and the Black Combe range across the Duddon Valley integral parts.

Leave by continuing north, initially, a good path rapidly making the drop to Goat's Hause. In the very lowest point a cairn to the right marks the start of the descent to Goat's Water. From this well worn path, most eyes will largely be fixed on the imposing buttresses of Dow Crag. At the bottom the path runs the length of the tarn's shoreline, at times literally hopping across water-lapped boulders. At the end turn to admire the cliffs one last time from so close a vantage point, noting in particular the deep gullies which we were earlier atop. A distinct blue object at the base of the crag is a first aid kit.

The path leaves the combe and descends into the amphitheatre known as the Cove, skirting round to the left to avoid its marshy centre. Up to the left are former slate quarries on the flank of the Old Man, and at the end of the Cove, traces of a green sunken way which once served them are met. The path now descends more firmly to rejoin the outward route. Dow Crag's mighty cliff disappears for good just before reaching the Walna Scar Road to retrace outward steps.

Brown Pike and Dow Crag from Cove Bridge

```
               SUMMITS
CONISTON OLD MAN   2634ft/803m
      BRIM FELL   2611ft/796m
      SWIRL HOW   2631ft/802m
```

START Coniston   **Grid ref.** SD 302975

DISTANCE 8 miles/13km   **ASCENT** 2900ft/885m

ORDNANCE SURVEY MAPS
1:50,000 - Landranger 89 **or** 90
and Landranger 96 **or** 97
1:25,000 - Outdoor Leisure 6

ACCESS Start from the village centre. Large car park. Served by bus from Ambleside.

Who does not know the Old Man of Coniston? One of Lakeland's favourite characters shares with Helvellyn and Skiddaw an attraction to people not generally accustomed to the high fells. No Lake District mountain has endured such an all-round onslaught at the hands of man as has this Man. The lower slopes bear fascinating evidences of copper mining activity, absorbing industrial relics somewhat over-shadowed by higher altitude slate quarries. Such is the resilience of the mountain that it can shrug off such blemishes and still project an endearing front.

S Leave the village centre by a narrow road on the south side of the bridge on Church Beck. This climbs to the *Sun Hotel*, immediately behind which a narrow, short-lived lane runs on to end at a gate at the last buildings. Already a great skyline hovers ahead, featuring Great How Crags on Swirl How. A broad track runs through the field, crossing a sidestream just above its confluence with Church Beck, then climbing above the main beck's wooded environs. The going eases out and the track runs on past fine waterfalls to arrive at Miners Bridge.

A path continues upstream, quickly reaching a gate in a descending wall. This is a superb moment as the majority of the walk reveals itself, with an imposing skyline running from Coniston Old Man's summit towards Swirl How. In front is Coppermines Valley, with the white-walled youth hostel prominent. Waterfalls on Low Water Beck and Levers Water Beck decorate the middle distance.

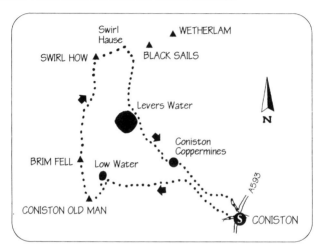

The path makes gentle progress up the slope above the valley, rising to a wall corner at the top then on to the last wall, just behind. Quarry spoil beneath us is just one example of the remains that will be seen. Continuing, the path rises onto an old quarry road. Turn right up this a matter of yards to a fork. Take the left-hand one which spirals steeply up to arrive at an extensive former quarry site. Looking back, Coniston Water is fully revealed, while beyond the coppermines are the pass of Swirl Hause and the peak of Black Sails. Pass through two level sections of ruins of stone sheds, with rusting cables and tramway tracks in amongst the spoilheaps.

Continue up to a fork, with a dark tunnel just yards to the left beneath a prostrate cable stanchion. Here bear right, quickly rising past the main quarry face and away from the site. A few steady minutes further, the path arrives at the basin of Low Water. This is a stunningly located mountain tarn, with the summit ridge brooding directly above. A recommended path runs on the few extra yards to the bouldery shore.

The final stage of the climb sees the path rising left, soon engaging a fine series of zigzags up to, unbelievably, more quarry evidence. These smaller scale workings are negotiated on part restored paths to reach more open ground. The path then treads easier terrain for the final few minutes to the immense slate platform marking the highest point of the walk. Just beyond it stands an Ordnance Survey column, and the whole is perched above the steep eastern face, offering one of the finest bird's-eye views, into Low Water. If looking elsewhere one cannot fail to be impressed by the two-sided picture. Inland rise the hills, a line-up of summits rather than a balanced mountain scene; the southern arc, meanwhile, depicts the decreasing foothills of south Lakeland, intermingled with lakes and tarns and culminating in an extensive coastline formed by the indentations of Morecambe Bay.

From the Old Man long strides are the order of the day, turning north along the rim of Low Water's combe, with a broad path on excellent turf leading to the solid cairn on Brim Fell. Little more than a stepping-stone between the walk's two major tops, Brim Fell also holds the dubious distinction of being the least interesting summit in this group of hills. A visit to the eastern slopes is repaid with a striking view down into the heart of the copper mining district; here the fell's rugged east face can be seen to conform to the general pattern of the group.

Continuing along the whaleback ridge the saddle of Levers Hause interrupts the climb to Swirl How. From this vicinity there are good views down over Levers Water to Coniston village and lake: this is also an escape route, as indicated by its cairn pointing to a line of cairns marking a steep, rough descent to the tarn. The short climb to the summit of Swirl How is playfully interrupted by the modest tops of Little How Crags and Great How Crags, still with excellent views down to the right.

In poor visibility it is important not to mistake Great How Crags for Swirl How: fatalities have occured in attempting descents east from here. Keep on along the ridge until gaining the latter's cairn, which even on a clear day only appears two minutes before reaching it across a tilted, stony plateau. Stretching all of seven feet into the sky, the unmistakeable cairn appears to teeter on the brink of an unbroken plunge to the Greenburn valley - this is the guarantee that you're on Swirl How. This is a grand place to be, for despite being marginally overtopped by the Old Man, Swirl How is undeniably the kingpin of the Coniston Fells, with ridges radiating to all points of the compass.

Within yards of the cairn, a splendid descent of the east ridge commences by way of Prison Band. This melodramatic name has induced numerous writers over the years to exaggerate its nature: though a heady mountain atmosphere pervades, nothing more than an occasional rock step is encountered. Ahead, Wetherlam initially appears subdued, yet as height is lost its addition as a tempting conclusion to the route seems less of a prospect! At the base of the ridge the neat, intervening col of Swirl Hause is reached.

Though the main path continues east to cross Black Sails' flank to Wetherlam, our path swings off right, bound for the waiting Levers Water. The path runs down to its shore at a very gentle gradient, indeed the opening section is merely a traverse across Black Sails' slopes, well above the stream. Surprisingly the path loses its way a little lower down, but the line is distinct enough to gain the rocky shoreline. Go left on a clearer path to the outflow, and descend a stony track. Initially very rough, it soon improves to pass beneath the brooding Kennel Crag up to the left.

With Paddy End Copper Works site below, the track reaches a hairpin bend. Advance straight on a contrastingly inviting green path, slanting down the bracken fellside and across a water cut (one of a series built to convey water from the becks to the mines). Coniston Coppermines appear below, and at a fork the main branch curves down to the right onto the old mine road, thence going left down to the hostel.

Restored buildings in the enclosure on the left include a heritage centre where it is intended to preserve reminders of the once thriving copper mining industry. Conclude by heading off down the long, level mine road through the Coppermines Valley. Simply remain on this to finish, passing en route the Miners Bridge which could of course be re-crossed if desired. Otherwise, the rough road drops down outside some extremely lively scenery as Church Beck tumbles in fine waterfalls down through a deep gorge. On acquiring a surface the road runs back into the village alongside the *Black Bull*.

The Coniston Fells from the south-east, with the Old Man and Swirl How sandwiched between Dow Crag and Wetherlam

93

TABLE OF SUMMITS

	FELL	FEET	METRES	
1	BOWFELL	2959	902	....
2	FAIRFIELD **M**	2864	873	....
3	CRINKLE CRAGS	2818	859	....
4	CRINKLES SOUTH TOP •	2736	834	....
5	SHELTER CRAGS •	2674	815	....
6	CONISTON OLD MAN **M**	2634	803	....
7	SWIRL HOW	2631	802	....
8	Brim Fell #	2611	796	....
9	DOVE CRAG	2598	792	....
10	Great Carrs #	2575	785	....
11	DOW CRAG	2552	778	....
12	HARTER FELL	2552	778	....
13	RED SCREES **M**	2546	776	....
14	GREAT RIGG	2513	766	....
15	WETHERLAM	2503	763	....
16	HIGH RAISE **M**	2500	762	....
17	ILL BELL	2484	757	....
18	BLACK SAILS •	2444	745	....
19	HARRISON STICKLE	2415	736	....
20	SEAT SANDAL **M**	2415	736	....
21	Sergeant Man #	2411	735	....
22	KENTMERE PIKE	2395	730	....
23	Thunacar Knott #	2372	723	....
24	FROSWICK	2362	720	....
25	PIKE O'STICKLE	2326	709	....
26	YOKE	2316	706	....
27	PIKE O'BLISCO **M**	2313	705	....
28	Pavey Ark #	2296	700	....
29	Brown Pike #•	2237	682	....
30	Loft Crag #	2231	680	....
31	High Pike #	2152	656	....
32	ROSSETT PIKE	2136	651	....
33	LITTLE HART CRAG	2090	637	....
34	Shipman Knotts	1926	587	....
35	Steel Fell	1814	553	....
36	Tarn Crag	1807	551	....
37	Blea Rigg	1775	541	....
38	Calf Crag	1761	537	....
39	Low Pike	1666	508	....
40	Stone Arthur	1652	504	....
41	Wansfell	1597	487	....
42	Wansfell Pike •	1588	484	....
43	Lingmoor Fell **M**	1538	469	....
44	Gibson Knott	1384	422	....
45	Helm Crag	1328	405	....
46	Silver How	1296	395	....
47	Loughrigg Fell **M**	1099	335	....
48	Holme Fell **M**	1040	317	....

KEY

For walkers who like their hills to be classified:
UPPER CASE - 2000ft fells with at least 100ft/30m of re-ascent ('HEWITT')
\# - minor 2000ft fells   • - non 'WAINWRIGHT' fells
M - fells with at least 500ft/150m of re-ascent ('MARILYN')

LOG OF THE WALKS

WALK	DATE	NOTES
1		
2		
3		
4		
5		
6		
7		
8		
9		
10		
11		
12		
13		
14		
15		
16		
17		
18		
19		
20		
21		
22		
23		
24		
25		

INDEX

Summits and other principle features
Walk number refers; Start points in bold